Exclusive Father of the Bride Speeches

By

John Wilson

Contents

Introduction

According to most studies, people's number one fear is public speaking. Number two is death.

Well well now that you have laid your hands on the best material available ever on the father of the bride speeches you can leave all your fears behind.

Thank you for your purchase and many congratulations!

You can get set to experience the most entertaining wedding speeches you have ever read.

Also the book teaches you how to write your own father of the bride speech, just like a professional writer. You will also learn the tips and tricks of how to deliver a speech and make your presentation appealing.

It prepares you on both fronts: content and presentation, both being the equally important aspects of speech giving. You will find lots of selected, exclusive and very relevant toasts and quotations that can be added to your speech or used otherwise on the wedding day.

I am sure with little practice and by following whatever you learn from this book, you will sail through smoothly and make an impression on the wedding day. Your speech will be truly a memorable speech.

This is the day that you owe it to your daughter to make her feel special and make her realize just how much she and her happiness mean to you. It is the most important day of her life and you surely are an important part of this day. You just can't afford to let her down.

Here you will find a variety of speeches to pick and choose from. I have tried to include different varieties of speeches to fit and match different personalities. Please remember that you might not like all the speeches but you will surely find lots of material to suite your individual personality and style. There's something for every father of the bride here. At least that has been my attempt.

Lots of anecdotes and incidents have been used to add entertaining value to the speeches. Please feel free to replace your own real life incidents with these ones. There are many stories that you can surely relate to and might not even need to make changes. I have tried to keep the writing style such that you can easily adapt the speeches and integrate your own stories in them.

Hope you find this compilation as useful as many others have already found it to be. I would love to hear from you and make improvements in my work. Please leave me your feedback/testimonial and comments and share your experiences with me about the wedding day by emailing me on my personal email john@bestfatherofthebridespeeches.com

Your feedback gives me the motivation to improve thus giving a better output to people who need quality speeches.

Enjoy as you go along!

Father of the Bride Speeches

SPEECH 1

For those of you who don't know me, I am the beautiful bride Jane's father. A very warm welcome to all the family and friends that I have come all the way to be a part of such an important and special day of Jane and Tim's lives.

A special thank you and welcome to Tim's parents Amanda and Mathew. Hope all of you are having a great time.

We're here today to honor the union of my daughter Jane and her husband Tim; a union that, if I may say so, has been a long time coming.

It seems like only yesterday that my little girl, my sweet Jane, was staging mock weddings in our garage, at the tender age of 5. She would wear a modified plastic bag as a wedding dress, and assign either her favorite Ken doll or our cocker spaniel Irving to act the role of the groom.

Well, I must say that her new husband Tim is significantly taller than a Ken doll, and not nearly as hairy as good ol' Irving. And I assure you whole-heartedly that the dress she is wearing today costs much, MUCH more than a flipping plastic bag. (Pause for Laughs)

I also can say, in all honesty and with all sincerity, that Tim is a fine man who loves my daughter very much.

Indeed, Tim fulfills the dreams of my daughter—and the dreams of her mother and myself. Parents have dreams too, you know; we yearn for our daughters to find the men of their hearts; loving, faithful men who will love our daughters beyond all reason. Wise men, who join our daughters in making sound decisions for their families and future. Kind men, who will never hurt our baby girls.

In Tim, I truly believe Jane has found that man. He doesn't say much, but through his every deed and gesture he shows his dedication to our daughter. He hangs on her every word and truly respects her opinions, opening every door for her and comforting her in times of need. He makes her laugh, buys her silly little gifts (just as I still do for her mother Rose) and never forgets her birthday, or the anniversary of their first date. Now that I can't claim to do, as my dear Rose will attest. (Pauses for laughter). Tim is endlessly kind and courteous. Above all, he loves our daughter Jane beyond all reason.

And why shouldn't he? Jane is an amazing young woman; intelligent, beautiful, sweet, a credit to her mother and me. We've watched her grow from a freckle-faced kid with pigtails to a mature, dignified career woman. We've seen her grow in so many ways and— in the past four years—Tim has grown right along with her.

Jane and Tim met in college, where both were laying the foundations of their lives and careers. As Jane studied and excelled at school, she told us she had little time to date; but for Tim, she made time. She wrote glowing letters home about the charming, handsome young man who had stolen her heart. We got detailed chronicles of their first date, their first kiss (OK, for the record that one happened to be a little too detailed for my liking), and the evening that he proposed.

Just as I did with my wife years earlier (we don't need to get into exactly how many), Tim took Jane to a nice restaurant and got down on one knee to propose. Recently, on our anniversary, I myself tried to recreate the 'getting down on one knee' part. I was just afraid I wouldn't be able to get up again. (Pauses for laughter)

On the evening of their engagement, Tim presented Jane with a bouquet of flowers and a sincere promise for the future; a promise to love and honor her forever, above all others.

It was then I knew my daughter had made the right choice; that she had chosen a gentleman, just like dear ol' Dad. (Pauses for effect) Except substantially more handsome. (Pauses for laughter)

I somehow know that Tim is the man Jane has always dreamed of; the man she pictured beside her at the makeshift garage wedding, so many years ago. The man of her dreams. The man of her heart.

I welcome Tim with open arms into my family; the same arms that will remain open for my little girl, any time she needs me. For Rose and me, Jane is the true miracle of our lives. And we watch with pride as she and Tim embark on their own life. Their own miracle.

SPEECH 2

Hello everyone. I am the father of the bride Andrew William and on behalf of my wife Rose and myself I would like to thank you all of you for coming and being a part of such a special day for Jane and Tim.

I would also like to thank Tim's parents Amanda and Mathew, two wonderful people who make me feel that we are already a part of one big family. It is an absolute privilege and a joy to know you both.

Today we celebrate the marriage of my daughter Jane and her husband Tim. A nicer, smarter, more beautiful couple you'll never meet; and that, of course, is coming from a totally unbiased source. (Pauses for laughter)

When my little girl came to me six months ago and asked for advice about getting married, my reply was wise and succinct:

"Don't do it!"

Jane after all is my only daughter. And frankly, I wasn't quite ready to let her go. Not just yet.

Luckily, though, I soon got the chance to meet her intended. I found Tim to be a kind, intelligent young man with flawless good manners; he even pretended not to notice the sizable rubber baseball bat in my hands. (Pauses for laughter)

I had a long talk with Tim about his dreams and goals, and found that, like my daughter, he was an ambitious, goal-directed person; one who knew what he wanted and, just as important, how to go about getting it. He's well spoken and well educated. A real gentleman.

More importantly, he loves my daughter very much. From the moment he stepped into our house I saw the love in his eyes when he looked at Jane, the tender way he held her hand, the way he hung on her every word. My wife Rose, in fact, berated me for a week afterward because—in her eyes, at least—I didn't pay her the same kind of attention. (In a dry tone) Thanks a lot, Tim.

Seriously, though, I soon came to realize that—while I was letting Jane go—I was sending her to be with a man who would take good care of her.

Of course, I should have known my little girl would pick a winner. Jane is a woman of impeccable taste, class and great intellect. She's one of those annoying people who excels at everything, whether it's school, work, volunteer projects...her heart and mind are large and pure, and it's only natural that she'd excel in the romance department as well.

I used to think it was so corny to say that a couple was two halves of a whole; but in the case of these kids, it's really true. Jane and Tim complement each other in every way; they both have strong values and a solid moral code. These are traits they are sure to pass on to their children.

Aside from creating a beautiful family, I see Tim and Jane having an exciting life together; one complete with business ventures and creative collaborations, exciting trips, fun social events. These kids will see and do it all. And as long as Jane still makes time to come home once in awhile and visit Mom and Dad, that's just fine with me.

I realize these visits won't be frequent, though, as these two are a busy pair, always on the go. They're off to a play or a ballgame one day, a museum or conference the next. Despite this busy schedule, though, this couple always makes time for each other. No matter where they are, they find a corner that's all theirs; a place to hold hands, to talk, to kiss (of course, being Jane's dad I always look away during that part).

They make each other laugh, dry each other's tears, make each other think. Perhaps most importantly, they bring out the best in each other. Jane inspires Tim to be the best he can be, and he does the same for her. Of course, being my daughter, Jane was perfect already. (Pauses for laughter)

I'd like to conclude today by offering this couple some words of advice they probably don't need, as perfect as they are; but Jane is a good daughter, so she'll listen anyway. (Pins Tim with a glare of mock intimidation)

And Tim, if you don't listen, well, suffice it to say I still have that rubber baseball bat. (Pauses for laughter)

Kids, marriage is not a bed of roses. You will have arguments and you will disagree. Some days you'll wonder, "Why in the (insert favorite expletive here, Tim and Jane) did I marry this person?"

When you reach those times, and they will come eventually, think back to this day. Think back to the love you felt, the joy that ruled your hearts and minds.

And if all that doesn't work, give me a call Jane; I'd be pleased to bring over the rubber baseball bat.

All kidding aside, Kids; I'm so proud of you. I love you both. Congratulations and God bless!

SPEECH 3

Today we're gathered for the wedding of my darling daughter Jane and her husband Tim.

I would sincerely like to thank each one of you for coming over and being a part of this special day. I would also like to extend a special thank you to Tim's parents Amanda and Mathew for all your support. I would like to welcome you in our family with open arms.

A special thank you also goes out to all the organizers, staff at the hotel, the reception hall and church. Because of your efforts things have been going so smoothly today.

Frankly though I am shocked to be here. When she was a little girl, Jane always swore to me that she'd never marry. Unless, that is, she found the perfect man.

Her sister told her to keep dreaming. Her mom told her that, since she was perfect herself, her standards were just fine. I said, fine, whatever, as long as she wasn't still living under our roof at the age of 35. (Pause for laughter)

Well, suffice it to say Jane didn't let me down; then again, she never does. She went off to college, earned a degree, and established a great career. She also found herself the perfect man.

Tim is, in many ways, a mirror of my daughter. They're both intelligent, focused, ambitious people with hearts of gold.

I guess they were destined to find each other; to form this perfect couple that annoys everyone into a state of perpetual envy with their, well, perfection. (Pause for laughter)

I hope that I played some part in making my daughter the wonderful person she is today. I certainly did try; I read to her when she was little, kissed her bruises when she got hurt, and helped her with her homework. I taught her always to say, "Please" and "Thank you" and to listen when her mother spoke; a lesson I have learned myself, painfully and repeatedly. (Pause for laughter)

As Jane grew up, I also ventured to give her some advice for the future; whether she wanted it or not! (Pause for laughter) I told her that, when she chose a career, she should pick one she would be comfortable with, a job that would both challenge and satisfy her. An occupation that would make her happy.

And when she chose a man, I suggested that she use essentially the same guidelines.

When I met Tim, I knew that my little girl listened to my advice.

Tim makes Jane comfortable. He listens to her problems, gives her impromptu shoulder rubs, and always assures her that everything will be all right; even when they were planning the wedding, and Jane was having a full-fledged panic attack at every dress fitting and cake tasting. (Pause for laughter)

At the same time, Tim challenges Jane. He doesn't tell her what she wants to hear, but what she needs to hear. He makes her laugh and makes her think, in equal measure. And, though I'm sure Jane will throttle me for announcing this publicly, he beats her at Trivial Pursuit every single time they play. (Pause for laughter)

Tim satisfies Jane. If she's hungry, he goes to the kitchen to cook her a meal; or, if he's feeling a bit lazy, he'll head for the nearest fast food drive-thru (Pause for laughter). If she's had a bad day, he's always ready to cheer her up with a gift, a kind word, or a warm hug. He makes her feel complete; to me, that's the ultimate satisfaction.

Above all, Tim makes Jane happy. That daughter of mine has a beautiful smile; and since she met Tim, I've seen that smile a lot. Every day he fills her life with joy. Well I must give the credit to both Amanda and Mathew for bringing up such a wonderful son.

And from what I know of my daughter, she fills Tim's life with happiness too. As her mother Rose and I can attest, Jane makes everyone happy, with her smile, her wisdom, her infinite kindness. At the risk of sounding arrogant, my wife and I are proud that we brought such a wondrous person into the world, to bring joy and happiness to the lives of others.

Tim, I must say you're a very lucky man. You just married my little girl; one who has kept the wide-eyed idealism of her youth, while developing an intellect and sophistication that renders her a cultured woman. My darling little girl has grown into a wise, funny, sweet, beautiful woman. And now, Tim, this woman is your wife. Congratulations.

Jane, in Tim you have found the perfect man you dreamed of as a little girl. I have come to know him as a man of kindness and intellect, wit and sophistication. He is your equal, and he's the man of your dreams. Congratulations.

Never forget though, Honey, you'll always be Daddy's little girl. And today you've made your mother and me very proud. We love you, Sweetheart.

SPEECH 4

We're here today to honor the union of my daughter Jane and her husband Tim; a couple we all know and love.

Thank you everyone for coming over to wish the couple. Also a special welcome to Tim's parents Amanda and Mathew. It has been an absolute privilege and joy to know such wonderful people like you.

Of course, as Jane's father I've known her longer than most. And just as long as we've been father and daughter, we've been great friends as well.

When Jane was a little girl, you could always find us either fishing or at the movies. When she was 10, I took her to a comedy about a father of the bride.

In this movie, the father of the bride was a hilarious, bumbling mess. His daughter, by contrast, was calm, collected, sweet, and absolutely radiant.

Jane, you must have been paying attention when we saw that movie. You have grown into that woman. You're a truly beautiful bride, my dear; lovely, poised and perfect.

And, for better or for worse (if you'll excuse the terrible pun), I managed to morph into the father portrayed in that movie. Like the comic character we saw in that film, I am nervous, bumbling and rather uncertain about this whole wedding business. The only bummer is that I'm not as funny, as handsome, or as rich as the comic actor who played that part. (Pause for laughter)

Even so, this whole wedding affair still seems like a movie to me. My daughter is the leading lady; a beautiful, elegant bride. My son-in-law is handsome, dapper and cultured. He is my daughter's romantic hero. Together they exude both wry sophistication and pure romantic spark. They have a romance truly worthy of the silver screen.

Kids, I have two messages for you: 1. Congratulations. My wife Rose and I are proud of you kids, and we love you. 2. (after a dramatic pause) It won't last. (another dramatic pause) Now please let me clarify. Your marriage will last, I truly believe this with all my heart. But the glamorous, romantic component of your marriage will come and go.

Tim, you'll see Jane without her makeup and fancy clothes. You'll see her in childbirth, and when she has the flu. You'll see her when she grows old.

My daughter looks like she'd like to scalp me at this point, so I'll address her next. Jane, darling, you'll see Tim with messy hair and ketchup-splattered jeans. You'll see him when he's sick, and after a long day at work. You'll see him sweaty and out of sorts. You'll see him as he grows old.

Why, then, am I confident in saying that your marriage will last? I say this because, beyond being a beautiful couple, you're also kind and wise. I know that you'll approach your marriage with a steadfast commitment, and a true sense of unconditional love.

No matter what obstacles you face, you'll face them together; and though not every situation will come complete with a happy, Hollywood-style ending, you will use your wisdom and sense of fairness to find amicable solutions to every question and problem. You will prevail over every obstacle with style and panache; the same qualities you now wear on the outside will always be present in your character.

Moreover, you'll pass these traits onto your children; you will govern and nurture them with a firm but loving hand, and join together to present the ultimate examples of a life well lived.

You'll make great parents, Jane and Tim, and a wonderful couple. Your life together won't always be a fairy tale romance; but before you throttle me upside the head for saying that one too many times, let me hasten to issue an assurance: in one way or another, the spark will always be there for you.

Even at our age, I love to swing my wife across the dance floor, and catch her under the mistletoe. We still hold hands in public, much to the embarrassment of our children, and my wife never fails to catch my eye when she dresses up for dinner.

Tim, you'll always think that Jane is the most beautiful girl in the world. Just as her mother and I do.

And Jane, Tim will always be your romantic hero. Your leading man.

As I said earlier, your life won't always seem like a movie; and in a way, that's a good thing. After all, this wedding didn't cost millions of dollars to produce. Your marriage, in all likelihood, will last longer than a week; about twice as long as the typical Hollywood marriage. (Pause for laughter)

And, most importantly, your marriage won't end with a title card that reads "The End." Why? Because, Tim and Jane, you two are forever. Congratulations, Kids. We love you both.

SPEECH 5

Welcome everyone. As most of you know I am Andrew Smith, the lovely bride's father. As you all can imagine my head is overflowing with ideas and my heart is filled with mixed emotions today. Initially I thought I would speak impromptu as I really have so much to say. On second thoughts however I think it's better if I stick to what I have prepared as I really don't want to be stabbed by my daughter after the ceremony is over. (Laughs)

As the father of the bride I am supposed to give advice to the newly weds. So before I begin my big sermon, trust me it's a big one, (Laughs) let me thank everyone for coming over and making this day so very special for us. A special welcome to the new additions in our family, Tim's parents, Amanda and Mathew Smith. Wow knowing the two of them I realize that we couldn't have really asked for more. My wife Rose completely agrees with me.

Today we honor the marriage of my daughter Jane and her husband Tim. And as my daughter says goodbye to the single life, I realize that—in a way—I'm also saying goodbye to her. And for the second time.

I said goodbye to my daughter the first time five years ago, when she went off to college. And the same advice I offered her that day, I extend to my daughter now.

Daughter, be careful. Marriage is a difficult journey, one that comes complete with pitfalls and temptations. Proceed with caution.

Daughter, be wise. You'll face many decisions in your married life. Approach them with a sound mind and vibrant logic. The answer won't always be easy, but with patience and reason it will come to you.

Daughter, be flexible. Married life is always a compromise, and you'll sometimes be asked to make concessions. Do so with grace, all the while maintaining your dignity and individuality.

Daughter, be brave. Marriage isn't for sissies. Every day will bring new challenges, and you must be prepared to face them.

Daughter, work hard. It takes a great deal of effort to make a relationship work, day after day. The work will increase when you have children; but, as I can attest, so will the joy.

Above all, Daughter, have fun. You're about to embark on the adventure of a lifetime. Enjoy your married life, and life in general, to the fullest.

As I mentioned earlier, these were some of the same words of advice I offered to Jane when she went away to college. This time is a little different, though, as—when she embarks on this particular life's journey—she won't be alone. She has married a fine man; a man who she can count on to be careful, wise, flexible, brave, and hard-working. And, judging from the love and laughter I see pass between the two of you on a daily basis, you are sure to have a lot of fun as well.

My only piece of advice to Tim is and mark my words Tim, never ever forget this date. If you do trust me you will have to pay a big price for it. Learn by heart the date of Jane's birthday, the date on which you first met, the date on which you first held hands, the date on which you first kissed, the date you proposed and ofcourse the date you got married. Keep a calendar handy always. I forgot a few dates and I am still paying the price for it. (Look at wife and pause for Laughs)

Jokes apart, from the beginning I knew the two of you were something special. Both intelligent, charming and kind, you make the ideal couple.

Relationships are never easy, it's true, but you two make it look that way. You're always laughing, kissing, talking; you get along so well you make the rest of us mere mortal couples look bad! Stop it now! (Pause for laughter)

You share the same values and morals, both of which are strong. You share the same goals, and have already worked hard to form a strong foundation for your life together.

No one was surprised, Jane and Tim, when you announced your intent to marry. And we all look forward to seeing what comes next: your beautiful first home, your enterprising business ventures, your sure to be wonderful children.

Through your romance, friendship, and ongoing mutual affection, you've already established a strong foundation for your marriage. Now it's time to build on that foundation.

Build hope for the future. You have so many dreams, hopes and ambitions; you must always believe that your dreams will come true.

Build a storehouse of memories. Cherish every moment together, remember the little things; places you go, things you do. Even the bad memories will be useful, as they're learning tools for you.

Build a schedule that allows time just for you. Whether it's an evening at a concert or a relaxing weekend trip, or just a walk in the park, make time for yourselves.

Above all, as you build your lives together, know that you have a number of construction helpers nearby to assist you in any way needed. The same friends and family who are gathered here today will always be there for you. We love you, Jane and Tim, and we wish you the best of luck in the future. Congratulations, Kids.

SPEECH 6

Welcome all. We're here today to honor the marriage of my daughter Jane and her husband Tim. The very reason you are here shows that Jane and Tim are special to you. Most of you have known Jane or Tim for a long time.

As I glance through this room I can see people who attended Jane's first birthday, her graduation party, people with whom she teamed up and played silly pranks with and people with whom she went on Europe trip and more.

There are so many people in this room that I would like to thank personally. First amongst them are Tim's parents Amanda and Mathew. Two wonderful souls who deserve the full credit for raising such a wonderful son. My wife Rose and I couldn't have asked for more in our son-in-law or should I say now our son.

I'm so proud of my little girl today; and of the fine young man she married. As I heard my daughter and her husband recite their vows today, I couldn't help but notice that they already have fulfilled the promises they made at the altar.

As they stared with warm sincerity into one another's eyes, Tim and Jane promised to love, honor, comfort and cherish. And that's exactly what they've done, practically since the day they met.

I've never seen a more loving couple than Jane and Tim. They're always talking and laughing, kissing and hugging; in fact, dear ol' Dad would prefer to see a little less of that last part, especially in front of him (Pause for laughter).

Jane and Tim honor one another, in a variety of ways. They ask and respect one another's opinions, are never rude or impatient, and always seem to brighten in one another's presence.

Jane and Tim comfort one another in times of need. When Jane has a bad day, Tim cheers her with a joke and a hug. And sometimes with a really lame Daffy Duck impression. Jane always encourages Tim to talk about his feelings; not a favorite 'guy pastime,' to be sure, but he says, reluctantly, that he always feels better afterward. (Pause for laughter)

Above all, Jane and Tim cherish one another. They look at one another with such deep abiding love. They speak to one another with utmost tenderness, and share private words and jokes meant only for them; likely because many of them are VERY corny. (Laughs) They treasure one another; they share a true friendship and a great romance, both of which are truly enviable.

So long before they said their vows, this couple truly felt them. And now in their married life, they will live them.

I really don't have much advice to offer this couple. Rose and I already did our part, when we raised Jane to be a warm, responsible person who loves and lives life to the fullest. I see every day how well she learned her lessons. Jane has truly grown into an amazing young woman; one whose great wit and infectious laughter brighten the lives of those around her.

Even when Jane was a little girl, everything she did predicted her standing as a great wife. The way she nurtured her first puppy. The way she ran her first lemonade stand, strong and industrious. The way she bossed around her little brother when they were kids (Pause for laughter)

And just as Jane was made to be a great wife, I am well assured that the man she married today will make an ideal husband.

When Jane first brought Tim home to meet us, I noticed immediately that he treated my daughter like the queen she is. He opened every door for her, hung on her every word, and kissed her with alarming frequency (cringes in mock discomfort). Maybe tone down on that stuff just a little bit in front of the old folks, Tim. (Pause for laughter)

From the beginning they seemed like the perfect couple; and when they announced their intent to marry, it seemed that a flawless relationship has come full circle. It had evolved into a beautiful constant that will rule their lives for eternity.

Tim and Jane, as you enter into this new, golden phase of your relationship, the only advice I have to give you is both timeless and simply stated: Keep on keeping on.

Keep on cherishing each other. Place your mate above all others, and treasure every moment together.

Keep on comforting each other. In times of turmoil, a husband or wife is the ultimate refuge.

Keep on honoring each other. Heed each other's words, respect each other's decisions. Respect each other at all times.

Above all, Jane and Tim, keep on loving each other. Today you came together in a union of love; in the years that come you will grow and preserve that love. You will nurture that love. That love will take the form of your home and your children. And know that as that love changes it also stays the same; and stays forever with you. Congratulations. May God bless you both, abundantly.

SPEECH 7

Today is that wonderful day when my darling baby Jane will get united to the love of her life, Tim in holy matrimony and I, as her proud papa, couldn't be happier for her.

I can assure all my guests accumulated here today, that the couple who are being united in wedding bliss at this beautiful venue today is the smartest, nicest, most lovely and romantic couple you have ever heard of and of course, I am being very unbiased here. (Pause for laugh)

A very warm welcome and thank you to everyone for coming over from near and far. On behalf of my wife Rose and myself I would like to extend a special welcome to Tim's parents, Amanda and Mathew, two wonderful people who have all our love and affection.

The two love birds here are as much head over heels in love with each other as Rhett and Scarlet, but of course they mean a lot less trouble. (Pauses for laughter)

I still remember that cold snowy morning in the quiet chapel of our neighborhood church some 8 to 9 months back. My little darling Jane waited for me to end my catechism. There was a pale little glow on her face and a kind of suppressed, nervous excitement that I had noticed for the past few days.

Knowing my pet as well as I do (this is an aside – my pet cannot keep a secret from her dad for very long – be it a new heartthrob or a breakup or some school girlish secret), I geared up for some fearful revelation! (Chuckles!)

Maybe something like "Dad, you know, I am not gonna take up that offer at Debenham's for I have received a scholarship to study law at Harvard" or something equally scandalizing! (Pauses for laughter)

What she came up with literally stumped me for a few seconds and it took me a while before I could find my voice. "I love Tim, dad. We both love each other a lot and now we want to get married. I want to marry Tim, dad, and I am serious". There was that quiet light of love shining through her misty eyes. My heart sank! My heart skipped a few beats.

So my daughter had finally grown up and she was ready to leave me, for another man! I was no longer the most important man in her life! It seemed like the end of the world for a second that stretched like an eternity.

But then I again looked into her eyes, looked at that dewdrop glistening in her blue azure eyes and I don't know what happened afterwards, but I mumbled yes and here we all are, celebrating my pet's wedding!

I remember the first time I met Tim. He was tall, with impeccable manners and a towering personality. But he had a kind smile – a smile that lights up his face and which had lighted up my daughter's heart, as I soon realized.

The chap is a clever guy as well, didn't take offence when I spoke to him rather sharply and treated him sharply as well.

But as we got talking, I realized Jane, the dear little passionate and wise girl as she is, with equally impeccable taste in men, had chosen a perfect husband for her, who will always care for her, be understanding towards her, provide for her and give her emotional support.

Most importantly, I realized, he will never stunt her professional growth with those hackneyed displays of male chauvinism that Jane's mother always berates me about!(pauses to laugh)

I had to concede Tim was ambitious, hard working, honest, a simple and loving man at heart and completely devoted to my baby.

No one could keep her happier than Tim, with the fond exception of yours truly! (Pauses to laugh)

I also won't mind sharing a little secret today. I was actually jealous of Tim! You see, when I asked my pet, as she was leaving, to put on her jacket as it was cold outside, she shrugged her shoulders and quipped "Dad, I am a grown up girl now and I know how to take care of myself! Stop worrying!" But the moment Tim lovingly wrapped a shawl round her shoulders, she looked at him gratefully and lovingly out of those beautiful eyes of her and didn't grumble one bit! That moment I realized Jane was no longer her dad's pet, her allegiance had shifted to another man, she was a woman now and dad has to take a backseat from now on. (Sing out a tune of Madonna's Papa Don't Preach).

Laughs. Well, I was madly jealous, man! I felt mad at Tim first! I felt that twang in my heart, that pang, that feeling that something inside me snapped. And I realized that I had to let her go.

And so we arrive at this auspicious day and I wish this wonderful couple a very happy married life, but my dears, at the same time, let me tell you as an expert on marriage with more than 2.5 decades of marital experience, the path of matrimony isn't an easy one and struggles and fights and differences of opinions and yelling will make life at times very miserable. At many points in life, you will feel like getting out your marriage.

And when those blighting times scald your heart, just remember why you got married, why you fell in love with each other in the first place. And in case you two can't remember, just give me a call Jane and I will, for once, argue the case for my daughter, as hard as I can. After all, I am the first man in your life, no offence to Tim!

To put an end to kidding, I love my daughter and son in law and I am proud of both of you.

Congratulations! May God always bless you always. Love u both.

SPEECH 8

I, Andrew Williams of North Dakota or as I am better known by my honored friends and colleagues - Andy, knows like all other hapless fathers that a day will come when my little bird, now grown big, will fly from the nest.

All daughters, whether you want it or not, grow up suddenly (or so it seems), find their soul mates in a great man (this is an aside - but times are changing nowadays and daughters are getting hitched to female soul mates as well – pauses for laughter).

Well to continue the story, after finding the right man, they get married right away and leave the nest empty and a void in their dad's heart that never gets filled up.

The father of a bride also has to wish his daughter and son in law best wishes for the coming years – years filled with wedded bliss – and when this time comes, as it has arrived now, in my case, all that a father can do is to watch as a silent spectator and wish her the best in life. Today, at my daughter's wedding, I am going to perform this role.

Jane was always a bright, spirited, adventure loving, outgoing girl with an indomitable passion that was always hard to miss and a sincere earnestness regarding the things and ideas she believes in, and right from her childhood.

I am glad that she has retained these qualities in her adult life. She has always excelled in whatever she has pursued, be it sports or academics and I have always trusted in her implicitly – in the choices she has made for herself in life.

I have always been proud of her and today she has made me the proudest father in the world by choosing Tim as her husband. I couldn't have found a better match for her and the first time Jane introduced me to her beau some 4 years back, I instinctively felt that this is the guy – this is the one she should settle down with. A few long and short conversations later, I realized Tim had fallen for my daughter hook, line and sinker.

And I couldn't be happier, though I admit I was jealous, damn jealous of this new man in Jane's life. What bowled me over was the fact that Tim was honest, simple, an diligent hard worker with a healthy ambition and a thoroughly busy professional with a successful career. But that didn't stop him from resolutely pursuing Jane and taking care of every little need/wish of hers or from being polite to an old retired daddy.

Tim is humble and down to earth in spite of his high flying career and today I am sure he is the best person on earth to keep my Jane happy. In fact, I believe, in this particular department, Tim can give a tough competition to Mr. yours truly who had sole proprietorship to Jane's love and devotion so long! (Laughter)

There is reason why I say all these. Jane always had a problem with her weight – she hated being called plump by her school and college buddies and in spite of being a very strong and no nonsense girl – this weight issue always ate into her and bogged down her spirit at times.

But Tim accepted her the way she was and not only that, brought about a positive change in her. He inspired her to look at herself differently, motivated her to lose weight and in the next few weeks I was witness to the amazing change in her.

She started dressing well, she started taking care of herself, she became the free spirit she now is – she was completely altered. What's the secret, I asked her. She laughed and after some dilly dallying introduced me to Tim, her university friend.

And they have been together since that time, by each other's side, through happiness and sorrow. And though I regret to lose my Jane to another man (aside – oh Jane! Daddy is no longer the king of your heart! Poor daddy), I couldn't be happier for her. I couldn't be happier thinking it would be Tim who will accept my daughter as his wife and not some rogue and I thank Tim and his family from the core of my heart for accepting Jane into their family and making her the latest addition to their happy family.

As I round up my speech, I would like to thank Jane and Tim for making me the proudest, happiest daddy in the world. I would also like to thank all the guests and especially Tim's family for taking the pains to join the celebrations today and for attending this wedding all the way from Santa Fe. Thank you to all of you for helping my daughter's wedding to be such a magnificent occasion.

Although I can go on and on all day, I think I am becoming a bit of a bore and it is now the wedded couple's turn to turn the spotlight on themselves once more. Cheers to the bride and groom. God bless you both. Love you.

SPEECH 9

Good morning ladies and gentlemen. Today, at my daughter Jane's wedding I, Andrew Williams of Pennsylvania or Andy as I am fondly called, announce the pleasure of making the first speech since I am the father of the bride.

For the past few weeks I have been reading up and receiving countless advices on how to make a perfect father of the bride speech, how to bring the house down with my humor but not to mouth smutty jokes, how to keep it short and simple, remember all the names and thank them and so on and so forth. Phew!

But will you believe it, my esteemed guests accumulated here today, if I say, it has been some 26 years since I was permitted to say or announce something or simply talk without being interrupted by or disagreed with or ignored or laughed or ridiculed at by the female members of my family, namely Jane and her mommy? So I am not going to let go of this golden opportunity. Well, jokes apart, now let's get on with this speech.

First of all, I, on behalf of my family would like to give the warmest of welcomes to all the accumulated guests – friends, relatives and the most special guests – the groom and his family for joining us in this greatest celebration in our family. I know fully well that most of the guests here have traveled across the oceans to join this party and Tim's extended family members had to travel all the way from Greece to be here today. While looking around the hall, I feel like a dad on top of the world when I see how Jane and Tim are surrounded by dozens of friends and well wishers.

I have to admit today that I am the proudest father in the whole wide world to accompany Jane – the most stunning beauty in this celebration. Of course, I will be accused of being biased in favor of my pet, but I think Jane today, in all her bridal finery has outshone and outclassed all the lovely ladies assembled in this hall.

I am also tempted to share a few embarrassing secrets about Jane with the guests here, but as you all know, Jane, until recently was an intern in my accountancy firm and is familiar with more gossip about her daddy than I care for her to know. So I am drawing a truce. But it will suffice to say that my wife Rose and I are both proud of our accomplished little accountant daughter who was till her high school days, the naughtiest brat we had ever encountered!

I still remember the day when Jane, as a 10 year old kid tried to light a fire by herself and almost gutted our whole house and that of our neighbor's as well! And I also remember how Jane, as a child loved to tear my important office papers in the paper shredder and giggled in glee while I tore all the hair out of my fast balding head in despair! It seems incredible that this little devil of a girl has now grown up into a dainty woman and is ready to fly from our nest.

She has after all grown her wings and found her soul mate in Tim on whom she dotes like a worried little fussy mother hen. It amuses me to watch these 2 love birds frolicking together (of course I look away when they kiss, for they are in quite another world at that time) and it reminds me of the times I spent together with a toddler in frocks and braids smiling away at her daddy with a toothless grin!

I am turning nostalgic and it is but natural, but at the same time I trust Jane's choice in Tim for she is bewitchingly wise beneath her naughty demeanor and I am happy that Tim's family has accepted her with open arms as their daughter in law. Tim is the best match for her and I know, in my heart of hearts, will be able to handle her with his caring, patient ways and it also helps that he is supportive towards her career aspirations.

A better match couldn't be made in heaven and I shall conclude my speech by blessing the newly wed couple and wishing them all the best in the coming years. Let us now propose a toast to the love birds and raise our glasses to Mr. and Mrs. Smith.

SPEECH 10

Good afternoon ladies and gentlemen. For all those who are not familiar with me, I am Andrew Williams, Jane's proud dad and I would like to thank you all for taking the trouble to join in this celebration from near and far.

I know it has been especially difficult for Tim's family to attend this wedding all the way from Australia, but thank you a lot for coming and making yourself at home, it's much appreciated. I would also like to welcome Tim, his parents and his brother and sister, Andy and Anne into our family.

I personally feel Jane has found her perfect match in Tim and though we haven't known him, since he was in his diaper days, my wife Rose and I both feel Tim has all those qualities and more that one could hope for in a son in law and he has more than fulfilled our expectations.

I must congratulate his parents for providing him with such a good upbringing and he is one of the most well bred young gentlemen we have come across. Well, Tim is a wonderful son, as I can see and I hope he will be a wonderful husband to our Jane as well.

I had a gut feeling that I would get on with Tim when he asked me out one night to the local pub and asked for Janeie's hand in marriage. I felt completely in league with him when Jane, the passionate overreactor that she is (just like her daddy, it runs in our family)screamed and hollered at him one day and had a BIG fight and almost called off the engagement and poor Tim came running to me in panic not so long ago!

Apparently, Tim had gifted her a rice cooker and a mixer grinder to put in the kitchen. But Jane painted the whole issue in a post modernist feminist color and accused her would be hubby of being insensitive towards an educated woman's feelings, aspirations and not being supportive of her dreams!

In short she blew her fuse off and called Tim an absolute fool– an honor bestowed on my exalted bald head by my wife at least a million times in the last 30 years!

Well, I had to budge in and reconcile the warring couple and it pleased me to see that both the love birds realized how kiddish they both were and it warmed my heart to see that Tim didn't mind apologizing to Jane instead of turning it into an ego clash, the way I do at times.

But the best thing I like about Tim is that he is an foodie just like me and can well appreciate the finer things in life, say, my daughter for example!

And now for some marriage advice! Well, marriage is supposed to be an eye opener and a suffer – ring and what not! It's when you cease painting the town red and begin to paint the fences, ceilings and walls of your house!

On a more serious note, what I want to say to this couple is that marriage means adjustment on both fronts and Tim has to remember the 3 universal words or commandments – only, just and all.

Some great philosopher or fool had once quipped that you should never try to understand women – they are only to be loved. Tim, if you ever help around the house, you will never compromise your masculinity. History books show that women love men who can wash the dishes and chop up the veggies and drop the kids at school.

One final thought – love is perhaps not the first thing you need to make a marriage work, but it isn't the last thing either. There will be fights and quarrels and ugly showdowns, but the trick lies in overcoming these problems by giving in. Remember marriage is not about who is right, it is about accepting defeat even when you know you are in the right and keeping quiet about it.

Well, I am now sounding like the biggest bore in the world and I am sure Jane is humming "Papa don't preach"! Just a word more. I am the proudest happiest dad in the world today, proud of both my daughter and son in law. I wish you the best in life, now and always and hope all your dreams for tomorrow come true. So friends and family may I request you to join me to raise a toast to the newly weds. Here is to the health, happiness and love of both Jane and Tim. (Raise a toast)

SPEECH 11

Good evening everyone, for those of you who don't know me, my name is Andrew William and I'm the father of the lovely bride.

I'd like to thank everyone on behalf of my wife Rose and myself, for attending and making this a very special day for both families. A special thank you to Tim's parents Amanda and Mathew Smith, for all their effort and hard work for ensuring that everything flows smoothly today. I'd also like to thank everyone who has helped put everything together to make this a perfect day for my daughter Jane and son-in-law Tim.

It's great to see all and meet so many new people that somehow have been a part of Jane and Tim's life. I know that some of you have come a great distance just to be here and we all really appreciate that and hope you're enjoying yourselves. Again, thank you all.

It was a bit hectic all day, as you can expect, trying to keep everything together and remember what time this person is coming and where we're supposed to be, but that's typical wedding stuff and it all went off without a problem. We had a few moments but everything is great.

I'd just like to say that Jane you look absolutely lovely today. Everything about you is so elegant and beautiful.

You have really made me proud with that smile and the way you carry yourself not only today, but every day.

For those of you that aren't very familiar with my daughter, I'd like to let you know just how wonderful she is. If you already know her then this is old news for you and you can share in my sentiment.

My daughter Jane is a wonderful woman. There was a sparkle in her eyes from the moment she was born. Her mother and I knew there was something special about her, I guess just as every parent knows there's something special about their children. Jane always was a source of light in our lives, as she never actually switched off the lights before leaving the room. (Laughs).

Jokes apart, Jane is my world and I couldn't be happier to see her marry such a fantastic young man. I have always been proud of Jane's accomplishments in life- in terms of her schooling, her career, her attitude towards life, but I must admit, Jane has made me the proudest today, by choosing Tim to be her life partner.

Jane and I have always been best friends and I've always tried to be there for her; from the first day of school each year when I'd wait with her for the bus, and as she grew older, helping her with her science projects, taking her to volleyball practice, and moving her off to her college dorm to take on the world. We've always been close and she'll always be close to my heart. She has my heart.

Tim is already a part of our family. He comes home, switches on the TV, raids the refrigerator and eats all MY favorite pudding. How much I detest that moment. (Laughs)

Suddenly I feel I am no more the most important man in my daughter's life. I have been replaced by someone. It feels strange at times but there is a certain joy in this change and in this transformation. Well the only thing permanent in life is change and for me this change has brought in a new joy, a new son into the family.

I know that Jane and Tim will be forever happy with each other. There is nothing more special than to see your daughter begin her own family and take on the world with her new husband. I'm excited for the both of them and I know they'll do great things together.

Jane you have always had a strong handle on life and this day isn't evidence of anything different. You are a beautiful woman, a beautiful bride, and one day you will be a beautiful mother.

Congratulations again Jane and Tim. You have an entire world ahead of you to enjoy together!

SPEECH 12

Hello everyone. In case you don't know, my name is Andrew William and I am the father of the lovely bride. Doesn't she look beautiful?

My head has been overflowing with ideas and my heart with so many emotions and memories. I actually thought that I will be impromptu while giving my speech and will speak a lot of things from my heart. Well I can see it wasn't a very good idea as right now my head is blank. So instead of making a complete fool out of myself and embarrassing my lovely daughter, I would rather stick to what I have prepared. Please excuse me for using cue cards.

I hope everyone is having a great time. I would firstly like to thank on behalf of my wife Rose and myself, Tim's parents Amanda and Mathew, for being so organized and putting in all the effort. Also a special thank-you to all the family, friends and co-workers of both Jane and Tim for being here today. I know that some of you flew in and drove from long distances just to be here and celebrate with us. To you, we are very thankful and it is great to see you here.

I'd also like to thank everyone who played a role in putting this beautiful wedding together. I think that everything turned out great. It seemed like the women were going back and forth about the table settings up until the very last minute so I'm glad that they got that all ironed out and taken care of.

So, as I said, Jane, the lovely bride is my daughter and she looks so exquisite today. Of course, she looks great every day, but today she is looking extra pretty and you can tell by that smile on her face that she's well aware.

She hasn't always had that pretty smile though, there was a time when this little princess used to parade around the house with an extra large space in her smile where her front teeth had fallen out. I think we have pictures of that somewhere so if you'd like to see those come talk to me after dinner and we can all have a good laugh at her expense.

I remember she used to parade around the house trying to whistle through that gap, stomping her feet like she was in a marching band. She was almost as cute then, as she is now. I'll stop embarrassing her though, and save those stories for another day.

Jane is a very intelligent and multi-talented woman. Apart from excelling in your career and in horse-riding you always had the perfect sense of fashion. Always dressed to kill! Well you cooked also for the very same reason. (Laughs) Just kidding sweetheart.

I know that you are such a fast learner and whatever you have decided to lay your hands on, you have done very well. I still remember even when you were little you'd get underneath the hood with your dad and watch everything I did, always asking questions about why this was that way, and why that was this way.

And, now look at you. You have found yourself a great husband to begin the rest of your life with. Tim is a very special guy, too. We've gotten to know each other quite well over the years and I've come to learn he is a man with a strong character, mature, intelligent and I know that he'll take excellent care of my daughter. We welcome you and both Amanda and Mathew in our family with open arms.

Jane has been so excited for this day, so I hope that it's lived up to her expectations. I know that she's happy to see so many of you and she told me earlier that she wishes this day would never end. I told her, this is the beginning of the rest of a beautiful life for you and your new husband.

Take care of each other and all of the kids that come along, how ever many of them there might be. Would everyone please join me in toasting the newly married couple, as they begin the new chapter of their lives together.

We love you both. God Bless!

SPEECH 13

For those of you that I'm yet to meet, my name is Andrew Williams and I am the father of the lovely bride that you see before you. Well first I thought of memorizing my speech but I really don't want to make a complete fool out of myself so please excuse me for using cue cards.

It's really nice to see so many family members and friends who have come out to celebrate this wedding. I'd like to give a special thanks to those of you who made a long journey just to be here. Some of you have flown and others drove for quite a few hours. That means a lot to the families as well as the bride and the groom.

A very special thank you and welcome to Tim's parents, Amanda and Mathew. They have been a great support and we already feel that we are all part of one big family. It has been a privilege knowing them as friends and as part of our family now.

I would also like to thank the Maid of honor, the Bridesmaid and all the friends, co-workers and families of both Jane and Tim for making it such a special day for all of us.

I am sure Jane is pleased with the way things have been going today as all her hard work is paying off!

It seems like not that long ago when I was teaching Jane how to ride her bike out in the driveway. I'd push her down the little hill in our backyard which probably doesn't even seem like a hill to her anymore. She'd cry out of frustration but she'd hop right on her bike again and keep trying. Eventually she stayed on and pedaled off. We were both hollering and yelling.

Then, years later, it was time to teach her how to drive a stick shift. I think that was more difficult than riding a bike. We gave up after the first day and took a break. "Let's just give it a day to sink in," I said to her.

"Good idea," she said. We came back a couple of days later to the old dusty back road we were practicing on and after grinding the gears a few times she more or less got the hang of it. She still isn't the best driver in the world but that's okay. What she lacks in driving skills my daughter makes up with her smile.

Those are just a couple of little moments about her growing up. There have been so many moments in her life where she's made me proud. Where I've just taken a step back and looked at her and thought, "Wow, she is really something."

Today is one of those days. I am just in awe of what she's become. She is truly a special young woman and I couldn't be more proud of her than I am today. She's found true love with a wonderful young man and I know they are really anticipating the life they have ahead of them – the places they'll go, the things they'll see, the children they'll have, and all of the high and low points they'll live through together.

In Tim, we have found a son that we never had. He is such a warm, loving person, mature, responsible and focused. My wife Rose and I welcome you in our family with open arms and hearts.

I am told that as a father and also as a new father in law, I am supposed to give advice to the newly weds. Well Jane my advice to you is to communicate all the time with Tim and not just expect that he will understand what you want without you having to say it.

To Tim my advice is remember the age old saying: 'Women are meant to be loved, not understood.' If you follow this trust me nothing can go wrong. (Laughs)

Jane, I hope that you live your life to the fullest and that you never lose thought of this day with your husband. This is something to build on for both of you. Congratulations and never forget just how proud your father is of the woman you've become. Love u both.

SPEECH 14

When I look out at this small sea of people I see a lot of faces I recognize and a few people that I'm not quite sure I know. So, with that said, I should probably introduce myself. My name is Andrew Williams and I am the father of the beautiful bride. I hope that I get a chance to meet every unfamiliar face out there.

Also, as I look around I'd like to say that it looks pretty good in here. With that said, I'd like to thank everyone that had something to do with making this day come together. Everything looks great and I'm pretty sure everybody is having a good time.

I just have a few things that I'd like to say to my daughter and tell you all a little bit about my daughter and what kind of woman she is.

Jane, as you can all see, is a beautiful young woman. You'll also notice that she's gotten her looks from her mother Rose. Really, Jane you look stunning today.

One thing that I've always appreciated about my daughter is the relationship that she and I have had her entire life. Even when she hit the teen years she never became too cool for her dad. We've always been best friends and she's never been afraid to come to me with any question or problem she's having. For that openness I am forever grateful.

It's that openness and willingness to communicate even when the topics might not be the greatest that has made our relationship together extremely strong and worthwhile. That same sort of communication is going to be important in your new marriage. I ask both of you that you keep the channels of communication open.

If there is one piece of advice that I can give Tim after years of being married, it is never to forget the two most important words of your married life 'Yes dear'. Believe me everything else will take care of itself. (Laughs)

On this note I would like to share a short story with you. A woman once bought two shirts for her husband, one green and one blue. They were going out for dinner and the husband happily put on the blue shirt and got ready. When his wife saw him she asked anxiously, 'Didn't you like the blue one?' (Laughs)

Well Tim I am sure you will get used to it all soon! Jokes aside I would like to mention that what a great son Tim has been to us. He is already a part of our family. He gets along so well with everyone specially Jane's brothers Allan and John.

Well the credit must go to Tim's parents Amanda and Mathew for making Tim such a wonderful person that he is today. We welcome both of you in our family.

Jane and Tim are both beautiful, loving people and I really think you were both meant for each other. Jane is one of the sweetest people this world will ever know. I know that Tim fell in love with her because of her kindness and her sweet nature.

Make sure that you never forget how special this day is and all of the people that love you that are here to honor your marriage. Never forget to communicate to each other just how much you love each other everyday.

Both Rose and myself are confident that both of you are two responsible individuals, ready to take on the new adventures of your life and embark on this wonderful new journey together, as a team, as partners and as friends.

May God abundantly bless you both. We love you.

SPEECH 15

It's really amazing how things can seem so hectic but then it all comes together so nicely to create a perfect evening. I'd like to thank everyone that helped make this day such a special day for my daughter. Everyone has done a great job.

I'd also like to say thank you to those of you that spent a great deal of time just traveling to get here. That means a lot to all of us and we're so glad that you're here. A special thank you and a very warm welcome to Tim's parents, Amanda and Mathew Smith.

For those of you who are wondering who the heck I am right now, I'm Andrew Williams, the father of this beautiful bride. I see a lot of people that I know and a lot of faces that I don't recognize. Feel free to introduce yourself to me because I'd love to get to know anyone that's here to support my daughter and new son-in-law in their marriage.

There were a few moments leading up to the wedding when Jane was a nervous wreck about getting everything to come together. We wondered if she was going to have a nervous breakdown and throw in the towel and just go to the courthouse. Well, I've spent a lot of money on quite a few deposits, so I told her it's too late now, if you go to the courthouse and get married I guess I'm throwing one big party for myself with a lot of fancy decorations and a big cake. (Laughs)

That would have been fun, but she came around and gathered herself. And now, here we are.

This has been quite an emotional day for me. I think that most fathers with daughters will agree with me. It seems it was just yesterday that Jane was sitting behind me when I was riding the bike, was running to catch her school bus, was playing basketball and longing to buy shoes and clothes and all the girly stuff. I remember the time when she went with her friends for the Europe trip. She was away for a month but my wife Rose and I felt such an emptiness inside us.

Trust me giving away a daughter is not at all an easy job. But let me also mention that having a son-in-law like Tim has made it so much easier. We are confident that Jane is in safe and loving hands. We have certainly not lost a daughter but gained a son. Tim is such a talented, wonderful and warm person. We welcome you and your parents in our family with pride and joy.

I couldn't be happier for my little girl and that I couldn't be more proud of her. This is her day and her moment and she is shining. She looks so beautiful today I can hardly believe it.

For Tim I would specially like to say a few words. Man is not complete till he is married – (Pause) then he is finished! (Laughs)

Jokes apart, Jane you've found yourself a wonderful husband and I know that the two of you will in your lives to complete each other and begin your own family. Raising a family is an adventure and Jane, you're a prime example of what makes raising children so rewarding.

Ladies and gentlemen may I request you to join me to toast this wonderful couple today.

May God abundantly bless you both

May your joys be everlasting and your pain light

May you have a long, happy and healthy life together.

Congratulations!

SPEECH 16

Hello ladies and gentlemen and thank you for joining us on this wonderful day. The day has gone so well and it is clear that all the hard work and organization that so many people have put in has been worth it.

For those of you who don't know me, I am the father of the bride, Andrew Williams. I am a very proud daddy today. A few formalities before I get started. I would like to thank, on behalf of my wife Rose and myself, all the members of the wedding party for helping make the day run smoothly. I would also like to thank and welcome Tim's parents and his family members. It is indeed a privilege and joy to know them all. A special thank you to the Best Man, the beautiful Maid of Honor and also the lovely bridesmaid. You all made it such a perfect picture today.

Finally I would like to welcome my new son in law, Tim into the family and hope that he takes good care of my daughter.

It's a big day for both Tim and Jane and for the families also. I want to share a few thoughts with all of you on this beautiful day.

After all the confusion between 'will they....won't they' I am glad that we are here finally. Janey thanks for taking the right decision. Your mother Rose and I are happy that our years of effort to give you the right values and teachings have not gone to waste. You have used both your heart and your mind to take one of the most important decisions of your life. I am confident that Tim will never let us down being the wonderful person that he is.

I'm pretty sure my daughter wouldn't want me to tell you this story but when she was little she dreamed of being a bride. From the time she was three or four she was dressing up in her mother's clothes or wrapping a tablecloth around her and picking flowers from the garden. She would dress the dog up as the groom and make him walk down the aisle with her. Her brother would be the priest and at the end of the service he would say, "You may lick the bride". (Pause for laughs)

It was very cute to watch but by the time she got to 21 and we had been through several dogs it had to stop! By her early teens she began to make a scrap book of all the things that she wanted for her wedding.

She would take photos of places in the park where she wanted to have the service such as under a tree or across the bridge and stick them in her book. She would draw pictures of her dress and spend hours looking for the right shade of ivory. However when she decided to move out she left the book behind her so when she came to us and told us she was getting married, not to the dog this time, we got the book out and had a good old laugh.

Some of the things she wanted seemed a bit worrying, such as a biker chic themed wedding and to get married in the middle of the sea but she has taken one or two of the ideas and put them to good use. It seems that she has done so much to make this day perfect and yet she has taken it all her stride and kept calm while sorting everything out herself, we just footed the bill!

Jane was always so confident that she will find her prince charming when she grows up. Well her sisters and friends made fun of her and said that it's only in the movie world that people find a prince charming. It's certainly not a reality. Well, I am so happy and proud that Jane has proved everyone wrong by finding herself a prince charming. Forgive me for being biased but don't they make a great couple together? So much in love together, so perfect.

When I saw Jane walk down that aisle I couldn't help but shed a few tears. Maybe it was because I was no longer the most important man in her life or maybe it was because she was just so beautiful, probably a bit of both. All I know is that I hope that the Jane and Tim can be as happy as my wife Rose and I are. We have been married for 30 years now and although it sounds like a long time it has flown by in a flash. My one piece of advice to my daughter and her new husband would be to appreciate the time you have together and make the most of it!

So ladies and gentlemen if you could all join me and raise your glasses to toast the bride and groom. Let's hope that they make each other happy for a lifetime and they will always appreciate each other and love each other. To the bride and groom.

SPEECH 17

Well what a day this has been! Thank you all for joining us and I'm sure I'll be able to get round to have a chat with you all at some point through the day. I am Andrew Williams, the father of the bride and a very proud father indeed!

When my little girl came to me and told me she was getting married I knew it could only mean one thing - I was getting old! Before you know it I'll be a granddad and having to have afternoon naps, although that bit sounds quite enjoyable! There have been a few points in Jane's life when I've thought, "Oh God! My baby is growing up!" I think the first would have to be her first day at school.

Jane was so excited about becoming a big girl and going to school that she couldn't talk about anything else. When the day came she was ready before 7am and was waiting by the front door! When we got there however, it was a completely different matter. She cried and clung onto us because she was petrified. However once she got into the room and made a few friends she was fine.

The next time my daughter made me feel really old was her graduation. It was one of the proudest days of my life and it was great to hear her name being called out and watching her get her diploma. We had a party afterwards for all the family and I caught a glimpse of her across the room. When had the little girl who had clung onto my pant leg grown up? Did I blink and miss it? It sure felt like it!

After that it was when she brought home her first boyfriend. It not only made me feel old but made me feel very protective too! This guy wasn't the best looking nor was he husband material so when she broke it off two weeks later I was so relieved. The bit that made me feel old was the reason they broke up. "He was too immature". He was 25!

And now once again I am feeling my age made worse by the fact that all her childhood friends are here too making it worse! I remember when you all used to come round and spend hours in the Jane's room chatting about boys and now look at you, some of you are married!

As I look back so many moments flash in front of my eyes. Jane sitting behind me on my bike, running to catch her school bus, rushing for her tennis, going crazy to find a dress for her first date and so many such moments. These moments made my life worthwhile. Now as she is getting married I have an empty feeling inside me.

Both my wife Rose and I are a witness to this little angel in her frock mature into an intelligent, ambitious, kind, loving woman. We have done our best to give her the right values and teach her the difference between right and wrong. And the result is for all of you to see here.

Her choice of her life partner shows that she knows the difference between right and wrong. We are so happy to have Tim as a part of our family now. He gets along with everyone so well, especially Jane's sister Jill and brother John. Both Rose and I couldn't be happier with this new addition in our family.

Also I want to welcome Tim's parents Amanda and Mathew in our family with open arms. We really acknowledge the fact that you have brought up Tim so well and also accepted Jane in your family with such warmth and affection. I remember Jane telling me how nervous she was when Tim took her to meet Amanda and Mathew for the first time. She wanted to make a good impression and was so anxious and worried. She told me that the way she was welcomed in the house she felt completely at ease with herself within the first few minutes. She felt as if she belonged to that space.

Well can a father of a daughter ask for more?

Even though I am feeling my age, it is pushed aside by the feeling of pure pride that I have for my daughter. She has had her moments like every growing up child does, but I can safely say that she has turned out to be such a fine and elegant young woman. Whether that is all down to me or her mother is yet to be seen. I do notice that she tends to be my daughter when she's done something wrong and my wife's daughter when she's done something right! Atleast that is what her mother claims! (Pause for laugh)

And now I also have a new son in law. If anyone is wondering he is no comparison to the first boyfriend Jane brought home! Less piercings for a start. (Laughs) Well Tim as you start this new chapter of your life let me tell you about a survey that was conducted a few years ago. It revealed that the average life span of married men and unmarried men is the same. The only difference is that in case of married men life seems a lot longer! (Laughs)

Jokes apart I would once again like to thank all the friends and family for coming over today.

Ladies and gentlemen please join me in raising a toast to the happy couple as they embark into this beautiful new journey. To my little girl and my new son in law. To the bride and groom.

May God shower his blessing on you abundantly

May you live a long life together and have all you need throughout that lifetime

May the road you choose is smooth and your burdens along the way be light

May your joys be everlasting and may all your pain be light

Thank you!

SPEECH 18

Ladies and gentlemen thank you for coming today. I am the father of the bride Andrew Williams, and would like to extend a very warm welcome to each and every one of you for coming over and blessing the beautiful couple.

Today is a very special day indeed. Today is the day that I hand over my daughter Jane to our new son in law Tim to love and cherish for many years to come, unfortunately the bride doesn't come with any warranty and I don't do refunds although I may accept an exchange. (Laughs)

Meeting Tim for the first time was a daunting experience. Like every father I assumed that no one would be good enough for my daughter. I imagined him to be big, hairy and extremely smelly, no, I'm not sure why either. (Laughs)

I was preparing myself for the worst so when Tim walked through the door I was taken aback to say the least. My daughter has done a great job in picking her husband as he is an intelligent, funny, kind guy who would do anything for anyone and I would like to welcome him officially to our family.

Jane and I have always shared a very close relationship but every now and again there are things that a mother has to deal with. All that crying for days in her room when the spice girls split up really panicked me but luckily her mother was on hand to support her through the bad times.

My role in my daughter's childhood can be better described as more of a job than a role. This job was of a taxi driver, no, chauffer. Not a day would go by when I didn't have to take her to a class or a mall or a friend's house. I have even been known to extend this service to her friends! I think the most memorable time in my employment, I mean in her childhood was the time I was ordered to open the door of the car for her at a party!

Then as she got older I became more of a removals man helping her move house and lugging furniture up and down flights of stairs. I didn't grumble, it was my lot in life and now she has a new man who will do all this for her just as I have. Beware, she doesn't tip!

But for all the jokes and humor I have to say that I am actually very proud of my daughter and I only do all these things because I love her so much. Tim will soon understand that she has so much to give and I hope that he will appreciate all the years he has ahead of him sharing the companionship of my little girl. She will look after you, care for you and most importantly keep you on your toes!

If there is one piece of advice that I could give about marriage it is to talk. I don't mean "hows your day been", I mean talk about everything. Even if you think it might cause offence or upset the other person, it is better than bottling it up and letting a small problem manifest into a huge issue. It may not be the easiest thing to do all the time but without communication you soon become two people who live in the same house rather than two people who share a loving relationship.

Before I end I would like to express my most sincere appreciation for Tim's parents Amanda and Mathew Smith. They have not only given Tim the right values and made him such a wonderful person that he is today but have also accepted Jane into their family with open arms. Both my wife Rose and I truly acknowledge this and welcome you to be a part of our family.

Once again I would like to thank everyone for all your support and help to make this day so beautiful. A special thank you to the Maid of Honor and the Bridesmaid for taking such good care of my daughter and for the wonderful job you did today.

I would also like to extend my gratitude to the staff at the hotel, reception hall and church for ensuring that everything runs smoothly today.

Now I'm done waffling on I only have one thing left to do and that is to wish the bride and groom many happy years ahead of them. Tim please do take good care of my baby.

There lies a beautiful wonderful world ahead of you to explore. Go make the most of it. Together you two make a wonderful team. You will go on to make a beautiful home, wonderful kids, great careers and a great life for yourselves.

Congratulations and God bless!

SPEECH 19

Hello everyone. Hope you are having a nice time. I am the father of the bride, Andrew Williams and would like to extend a very warm welcome to each one of you. Thank you for being here today on this special day of Jane and Tim. On behalf of my wife Rose and myself I welcome Tim's parents Amanda and Mathew Smith who have come all the way from Australia to be with us today.

We are here today to honor the marriage of my daughter Jane and her husband Tim. This is a union that is not only blissful, but long, LONG over due.

(To the couple) What took you so long, Kids?! We were about ready to give up hope! (Pause for laughter)

Of course, there's a reason that we were so anxious to see Jane and Tim tie the knot. They're made for each other. Annoyingly ideal. Petulantly perfect! (Pause for laughter) Aside from Rose and me, they're the most ideally suited couple I know.

From the time she hit her teen years, I saw my daughter Jane go out on a number of dates. Some of the guys she brought home were OK; others I had to bribe, cajole, or physically chase away. (Pause for laughter)

Ultimately, I never thought that any man would be good enough for my darling daughter.

Then, as usual, the little smart Janey had to go and prove me wrong. She brought home a young man almost as wonderful as she is.

Tim is a bright, ambitious young man who also has a great sense of humor; he laughs at all of my jokes, which in my mind proves that he does indeed have a stellar sense of humor. (Pause for laughter) Most importantly, he treats Jane like gold. I am both pleased and proud to welcome Tim into my family. And also Tim's parents Amanda and Mathew. I must say both of you deserve the full credit for raising such a wonderful son.

I know Tim appreciates this as an honor to be a part of our family; as everyone knows, my family is very tight knit. My wife, daughter and I are the Three Musketeers; we talk about everything and spend much of our time together. Jane is sweet, fun-loving, and my wife and I are proud to call her our best friend.

And we gladly welcome Tim as the fourth member of this exclusive social group. He and my daughter make a great team. They share similar interests and are fun to be around; I know there will never be a shortage of whoopee cushions and joy buzzers around their house. I know that, in equal measure, there will never be a shortage of love and laughter in their home.

Tim and Jane are great friends. They love to go to movies and ballgames, they share unforgivably corny jokes, and they face off regularly at tennis matches and all-night video game tournaments. (Casting a suspicious glance towards the couple) At least Jane tells us that they're playing video games all night.

Out of this friendship has arisen a beautiful, heartfelt romance. Tim approaches every date with my daughter like its Valentine's Day. He brings her flowers and candy (most of which she refuses to share with me!), and takes her to nice restaurants. Jane always puts on a beautiful dress for her dates with Tim; (cringes) though I assure you, none of them were quite as expensive as the one she's wearing today. (Pause for laughter)

As I said earlier, welcoming Tim into my family is like welcoming a new friend. So, Tim and Jane, let me finish today by giving you some advice from a friend.

Keep laughing, Kids. No matter what life throws at you, throw it back for criminy's sake! (Pause for laughter) And keep laughing.

Always remember to dance and enjoy the music. Life is short; enjoy every moment. Dance at your reception, dance at your anniversary parties, dance in the frozen food aisle at the Stop'n'Go...but only if it's really late at night and absolutely nobody else is around.

Stay strong. Marriage is a joyous journey, true, but it's beset with constant challenges, concerns and temptations. Stick together, stand firm, and you'll do just fine.

Above all, Tim and Jane, love each other beyond all reason. And if you're ever tempted not to, just stop and think about how happy you were on this day, at this special event (dramatic pause), and, Jane, just how much money this wedding cost your mom and me. (Pause for laughter)

Seriously, though, Tim and Jane, I can't tell you how proud I am of you today. As a father, as a friend, as the person who paid for this wedding (pause for laughter), I take such great pride in the accomplishment of your marriage. You truly are the perfect couple. I congratulate you, and I love you both.

SPEECH 20

Well ladies and gentlemen no groaning please because it is time for my speech. For those of you who do not know I am the father of the bride, Andrew Williams, commonly known as Andy and this is both a joyous and saddening day for me as I lose a daughter but gain a son.

First I thought I will memorize my speech but then I have so much to share and my memory retention being so sad I thought it would be better if I rely on the cue cards. So please bear with me. I plan to keep it simple and short because of my throat- you see if I keep yakking my wife Rose threatens to cut it. (Laughs)

I want to welcome all of you and also thank you for being a part of such an important day of Jane and Tim's lives. I know some of our family and friends could not make it today but they have sent their best wishes and I really want to express my appreciation for it.

Tim's parents Amanda and Mathew are welcomed in our family with open arms and hearts. It has been an absolute privilege and joy knowing them as friends and now as family. I want to specially thank both of you for all your hard work and effort to make sure that the day passes on smoothly.

When my daughter came to me to tell me that she was getting married taken aback as I never really realized that she has become such a big girl. The thought took me back to her childhood and how she has grown up over the years. It seemed like only yesterday that she was playing in the garden with her dolls and today she was telling me that she was now old enough and mature enough to get married.

I still remember the first time I met my new son in law he was nervous to say the least. He came to our house with a bunch of flowers for my wife and a very sweaty hand shake for me! I took to him instantly and knew that my daughter had made a good decision. I wanted only the best for my little girl and I think it is safe to say that she has chosen very well.

Now the day has come and we are all here today celebrating the union of the bride and groom. In the tradition of weddings and speeches it is down to the father of the bride to say a few words of wisdom with regards to marriage. My wife gave me lots of helpful hints on this part, mainly because she was petrified that I would embarrass her. So instead of saying what I believe to be the success to marriage and risk sleeping on the sofa, I am going to tell you what my father said to me on my wedding day.

I was so nervous on my wedding day. My father came to see me before the ceremony and said, "Son, there is one thing that you should always understand, something that you should always remember in your years of marriage. That one thing is that your wife is always right. These words will stand you in very good stead for the years ahead and will give you a very happy household."

Well unfortunately I didn't always follow my father's advice and now I am glad I didn't. For the whole of my married life Rose and I have been very honest with each other. We may have had our disagreements, we may have not spoken to each other for several hours but we have an open and happy relationship. Neither of us pretends to be right or wrong and we have a happily equal relationship which I hope will continue for another 25 years.

So now comes the time to toast the bride and groom but before I do I would like to say a few words to my daughter. I have always been so proud of you and today is no different. Seeing you in that beautiful dress has made my life complete and I am so pleased that you have found someone who makes you so happy. I love you my little girl.

Now I am only left to say one more thing. To the bride and groom!

May God shower his blessing on both of you abundantly and forever.

SPEECH 21

Hello ladies and gentlemen. I would like to thank all of you for joining my daughter and son in law on the day that they commit themselves to each other for a lifetime of happiness.

I am the proud and honored father of the bride, Andrew Williams and this is my time to shine and to tell you all about the awful things that my daughter has done over the years, only kidding! Just one or two awful things!

My daughter Jane had a wonderful gift for embarrassing my wife and I whenever we were out. If she wasn't shouting and pointing at the fat people, she'd be trying on skimpy underwear in the department stores. I wouldn't mind so much as she was only 7!

She just managed to always say the wrong thing at the right time and no matter where we went she would find some way to embarrass us. One day I had enough and informed my wife that when her wedding day came, revenge would be sweet and she would be shown the real meaning of embarrassment!

The only problem is that I can't really think of any embarrassing stories, other than her fashion disasters! When Jane was at her partying stage it was the late 90's. Shoulder pads were out, perms were out and platforms were in.

I seem to remember falling over several pairs of platforms not because I was wearing them but because they were always scattered around the porch!

One of Jane's major fashion disasters has to be her punk/Goth stage. She was never seen outside the house without thick black eye liner and leather boots with the most enormous buckles on them. She would spend her days in her room listening to Nirvana and writing in her journal.

She had some very unsavory boyfriends through these years and her mother Rose and I took to hiding the good china whenever they came round. They seemed to follow the same pattern of long hair (usually unwashed), oversized clothes and only able to speak with a grunt. As you can imagine we were quite relieved when the black clothes went away and the boyfriends became a bit more presentable!

Then came Tim. He was no comparison to the others, he washed for a start! He was polite, helpful and even gave me a hand fixing the car! It seemed that Jane and Tim really hit it off and I was pleased that she had found someone to make her happy. With time both Rose and I discovered that Tim has lot of marvellous qualities.

He is intelligent, mature, focused, warm, friendly and overall a great human being. Someone who would always love our daughter and bring a smile on her face. I must give the credit for this to Tim's beautiful parents

Amanda and Mathew for bringing up such a wonderful son.

When it came to the engagement Tim asked me for her hand in marriage so we knew before she did! To say that she was shocked was an understatement. She was furious that we had managed to keep the secret to ourselves!

Now the day is here and I think you will all agree with me that she looks absolutely stunning and that her dress was worth every penny in my opinion, even if it is only worn once!

The service was spectacular and both the bridesmaids and the ushers looked very smart. Thank you everyone. Thank you especially to Amanda and Mathew and all the friends and family present. Your presence means a lot to us.

Also I want to thank the staff at the hotel, reception hall and church and the caterers for the delicious food and service. Everyone has really put in great amount of effort and Rose and I really appreciate it.

I really want to wish the newly married couple a lifetime of happiness and luck. Let's hope that in 25 years time we will all be re-united again to celebrate their 25th wedding anniversary.

So can you please join me in toasting and raise your glasses to the bride and groom. May you have all the happiness in the world.

Congratulations and love you both!

SPEECH 22

Well what a day! Who would have thought you could get so much taffeta and so many flowers into one room! I would just like to say that I am very grateful that no one got hurt when throwing the bouquet.

The last wedding I went to several women left with black eyes while another was taken to the emergency room! For those of you who are thinking "Who's this bozo?" I am the father of the bride, Andrew Williams and it is my duty to address you all with a speech full of wit and humorous anecdotes.

Unfortunately my wife Rose helped me write this speech so we will be in store for neither humor nor wit but maybe a little moaning, she's very good at that! (Pause for laughs)

Rose and I have always been very proud of our children. We have a beautiful girl, Jane who happens to be the most stunning person in this room today, and we also have a son, John. But today we have become 5 as we introduce the groom into the our family and I wish him all the luck in the world as our thanksgiving games night looms round, you're going to need it.

Seeing as this is my one chance to boast about my daughter in front of a room full of people who have no choice but to listen I will make the most of this opportunity. Now I am not biased, but Jane has to be the most beautiful and intelligent woman I know. Oh, hold on, there's something scribbled here. What does that say? Apart from my wonderful wife? Must be a typo....sorry about that.

So where was I .....Jane... yeah Jane has achieved so much in her life so far and has huge ambitions for the future.

And Tim is such a great pal. He is mature, intelligent, focussed, kind and warm and also really in love with our daughter. But most importantly he is a keen sports fan which suits me down to the ground. We will often spend an evening watching the game, drinking beer, being nagged by Rose to put them on a coaster; it's just not manly is it? And while we're on the subject, for any wives out there who have sports fan husbands, no, we can't turn it down. It needs to be that loud otherwise we may miss something and have to watch it all again when it is repeated.

Here are a few words of wisdom that I would like to give to my new son in law. Number 1. Pick up your dirty socks. It doesn't take long and she won't nag you. Number 2. Put the toilet seat down. It doesn't take long and she won't nag you. Number 3. Listen! This one may take a while and they will probably be nagging you about not doing the first 2 right.

I also have a few words of wisdom for my wonderful daughter. Number 1. Don't bother nagging; he won't pick up his dirty socks. It's a man thing, we just can't see them. Number 2. Please put the toilet seat up when you're done. It makes your life a lot easier. Number 3. We ARE listening. Just because it looks like we aren't or we're watching a game at the same time doesn't mean we aren't taking in everything you are saying. Following these guidelines will make you both very happy and will keep the peace for years to come.

Well jokes apart knowing Tim for such a long time I am assured that he possesses all the qualities to keep Jane happy and give her the life she truly deserves.

I want to thank each and every one of you for coming over and making this day even more special. A special thank you to Tim's parents Amanda and Mathew for all your support and hard work for this day. I really feel that we are all a part of one big family.

Thank you to the Best Man, the bridesmaids and the Maid of Honor for making the service look so beautiful and spectacular. Rose and I really appreciate all the effort put in by so many people to make today's day so beautiful and special.

Now it gives me the great honour to toast the bride and groom to many happy years ahead of them. I can tell that they have a wonderful future ahead of them. So can you all please join me in raising your glasses to the bride and groom.

God bless you both. We love you.

SPEECH 23

It is my daughter's wedding today and ladies and gentlemen, as the father of the bride; I have the privilege to give out the first speech of the day. But before I start my long story cut short by editors (guffaws), I would like to thank all my guests and especially Tim's family for taking the pain to attend this wedding from near and far and I would like to welcome all of you gathered here today to Jane and Tim's wedding.

I also want to welcome Tim's mother and father, Amanda and Mathew and his brother and sister, Robert and Jill as well as the rest of their relatives and friends. It feels lovely to see how the bride and groom are surrounded by friends and family, all ready with their blessings and best wishes for this wonderful couple. I would also like to put in a special say of thanks to the best man and bridesmaids for the trouble they have taken to make this wedding a success.

But in the midst of all this merrymaking and revelry, we are sad to announce that Jane's granny and grandpa couldn't make it to this wedding from Adelaide because of their old age and ill health. We are missing you and we are also missing Jane's aunt Ruby who passed away a year back! But not to worry, just after this wedding, Tim and Jane will be traveling to Adelaide to take their grandparent's blessings. I am sure they will be really excited and happy to receive Jane and Tim.

I feel very pleased to formally welcome Tim into our family today though it has been simply ages since we first got introduced to him some 8 years back. And since I have been seeing this couple – Tim and Jane for the last 8 years, inseparable as they are from each other, I know what a deep bond exists between them and how deeply they feel for each other.

The fact that Jane is the most special person in Tim's life and vice versa is very evident and anyone can understand after a cursory glance what a made for each other couple they are! I personally feel they are the most wonderful and well matched couple I have ever seen, although I know this sounds very clichéd.

Jane in her designer bridal gown is looking like a million bucks! It feels incredible to think that the toothless little mite of a baby whom we called Jane has now grown up into a lovely and wonderful woman, strong, kind, ambitious, successful with a magnanimous heart – a girl who always loved athletics and won all the sports events in her school and college days.

But at the cost of being berated by Jane, let me just share this embarrassing little secret with you. Though Jane's marriage is leaving me with a sense of emptiness yet it brings me a certain amount of relief also. At least it will save me from all the car troubles that I have been getting into recently.

Jane is no doubt a very successful and enterprising fashion designer, who has won several design awards, but she is a complete mess when it comes to driving a car! She has been trying hard to learn driving for the last two years but not a day has passed without her bumping into the lamppost or the gate or into other people's cars parked outside the grocery store! Her car now looks likes a battered box of metal with broken tail lamps and headlamps falling off, but she refuses to back down! Now Tim be ready you have to handle the troubles now. Just kidding sweetheart. You know you can count on me whenever you want and let me tell you that I am amazed at your undying spirit that refuses to give up! I am sure you will master driving also soon.

I also remember our first tryst with Tim as he lay sprawling on the ground beside the drain one night singing "Jane I love you" at the top of his drunken voice and what a ruckus it led to thereafter! Tim was intoxicated so he wouldn't remember but I hauled him up and gave him a sound thrashing for being such a good for nothing lout and yet daring to date my daughter! It was a pity that Jane was not at home to appreciate all the troubles Tim took to propose to her! (Laughs)

But on a more serious note, Tim, in spite of a very unique first impression is the best match for her as he understands and handles her so well and it makes me so happy to think that he makes more sacrifices for her than she does for him! Well, I guess times are really changing and I have been constantly nagged by Jane's mommy Rose for being insensitive and selfish ever since Tim came into our lives. (Laughs)

Well Tim is a wonderful guy and already so much a part of our family. He is intelligent, mature, focused and fun loving. Both Rose and I are proud to call him our son.

Suffice it to say, I love my daughter and I am proud of the choice she has made and I love and am proud of both my daughter and my son in law and I bless them both. Let us now raise a toast to this wonderful couple. Oh! This must be a very sentimental wedding – they have even made the cake in tiers! (in a tone of mock surprise)

SPEECH 24

Ladies and gentlemen, wish you a very pleasant and sunny good afternoon! Well it better be sunny for this is an open air wedding venue and I don't want the rains to turn this wedding party into a slush and slime party! (In a tone of mock worry). Well, since I have been blessed with the memory of a geriatric goldfish although in shape I resemble an elephant (I wish I had its memory power as well, poor papa needs it), I decided to go for an autocue to deliver this speech today.

But my family members informed me that they couldn't stretch the budget that far! And then suddenly I experienced a moment of epiphany and this piece of paper (suddenly fishing out a paper) seemed good enough!

As the father of the bride, I would like to welcome and thank all the guests accumulated here today to celebrate this beautiful and momentous occasion of the wedding of Jane and Tim. I would also like to welcome Tim's parents, grandparents, uncles and aunts into our family and we just hope that over the years we will get to know each other better. I want to thank Tim's family as well for traveling down all the way from Michigan to Florida to attend this wedding and helping to make it a success.

Without your valued presence, this wedding would have been really incomplete. Thank you all for gathering here this afternoon to bless the beautiful bride and groom, it is much appreciated.

When Jane first announced that she was going to marry Tim in November, I wasn't a bit surprised but I could hardly understand why the rest of the family suddenly was in an uproar about the arrangements! Arranging a wedding is the easiest thing in the world – just hire a wedding planner and bingo, everything will happen smoothly.

Really, these women create too much of a fuss over tiny things. But I was very disappointed when Jane and my wife Rose dismissed my suggestion of arranging the wedding in our garden shed with one angry frown! However, to call a truce, I like this present venue a lot and it is perfectly fine by me!

And now comes the time when I am supposed to let a few embarrassing secrets tumble out of the closet! Well, Jane has almost been a perfect daughter, an epitome of goodness right from her childhood. (Smiles mischievously) And so there aren't very many things to say about her except that as a 6 year old child, she once took the goldfish out of its bowl and fed it to the cat which was all too happy to gulp down this unexpected treat! And once she had put marbles and pins inside my shoes that made me yell out like a man on fire!

Jane was always a great bathroom singer and one night she decided to be a bedroom singer as well and was singing away at the top of her voice at 2 in the midnight, blissfully unaware that her mommy and daddy were wide awake at this high decibel disturbance of their night's sleep. To make matters worse, her pet dog Ruffles (he's now dead, dear soul) had joined in the party and the two were having a rocking time together, screaming and howling at the dead of night! I got a mini heart attack that night.

And then she never failed to shock us out of our wits by bringing in a steady stream of grungy boyfriends. Well, anyway, it will suffice to say that my darling has inherited all her dad's quirkiness, but I am glad that she has also inherited her mommy's practicality and in Tim, she has found her most perfect, decent and best match. I ought to be grateful to Tim for taming this shrew and making her see reason!

Both Rose and I are so proud to have Tim as a part of our family. He helps Rose with watering the plants, gives me a hand to fix my car and helps Jane's brother John with his football matches. He is so much a part of us already and we really look forward to spending more fun times with both of you.

Together, Tim and Jane make a wonderful couple, completely clued into each other and totally made for each other and I am very proud of both of them. I wish them all the best in life, now and forever. Congratulations! Love you both. God bless you!

SPEECH 25

Good evening ladies and gentlemen. On this beautiful occasion of my daughter's wedding, I would like to welcome all my guests and thank them for taking the trouble to attend this wedding in the picturesque locale of Hawaii. I would also like to thank Tim's family for traveling all the way down from Glasgow to Hawaii with all their extended family members. It is my pleasure to welcome Tim, his parents Amanda and Mathew, brother George and sister Annie into our family.

I am also very grateful that Amanda and Mathew deemed my daughter Jane worthy enough to be taken as their daughter in law and we are all very happy at this union where not only two hearts are getting united, but where two families are getting united into one big happy family.

And of course, not to forget the best man and the bridesmaids, without whose valued contribution, this wedding wouldn't have been either complete or successful. Before I forget to mention, both Amanda and Mathew chipped in to make this grand Hawaii wedding even more gorgeous and we are all hugely indebted to Tim's family at their generosity.

I feel very proud and happy to see my Jane grown up and dressed in her bridal attire, ready to be taken away from me. I am really at a loss for words now, as I see this beautiful couple, Jane and Tim who love each other unconditionally and are extremely understanding and caring towards each other.

All those fond childhood memories are flooding my mind right now. The first day when I saw Jane– a tiny little 3 day old doll (I couldn't be present at her birth as I was away on an official tour) wrapped in towels! I can never forget that moment when I first held Jane in my arms cautiously, almost scared that I would drop her. A tiny little bundle of joy that just lit up my life with one toothless smile!

And I can still remember her first day at school, the day she learnt to walk, the day she called out for the first time "mamma" and then after a few days "papa"! It was one of the most inspiring moments of my life – one that I still cherish and in the coming years I will cherish this moment where I behold my Jane looking deeply into the eyes of Tim, the love of her life.

I remember how one night Jane– the soft little girl that she always was got lost in the woods where she had gone out on a picnic with high school friends. I almost had a heart attack, but thankfully she was found soon enough and we heaved a sigh of relief!

I also remember how she got injured in a car accident a few years back and was gallantly saved from the jaws of death by a dashing young man who also stole her heart along the way! Yeah, folks, you guessed that right, that man is the one she is going to marry today – Mr. Tim

Smith – a very hardworking, ambitious, simple and enterprising architect who has always been by my Jane's side ever since! I couldn't be happier with Jane's choice of life partner and my wife Rose and I will always remain grateful to Tim for saving our daughter's life.

At the cost of sounding clichéd, a happier and better matched couple I have never seen and I love her and am proud of her, proud of her intelligence, nobility, hardworking and ambitious nature, simple playfulness and I admire the way she adores her husband.

But all said and done, I will still never eat anything prepared by my daughter, not at the cost of my life. The lamb chops and broccoli that she prepared a month back will forever remain etched in my memory and it is now Tim's turn to be turned into a tester for her culinary experiments. So beware Tim, don't blame me and complain that I didn't warn you beforehand!

On a more serious note, I want to bless this couple and tell them just how much I love them both and I am extremely proud of both of them. May I request you to join me to raise a toast to the health, happiness and long life of this lovely couple? Congratulations kids!

Father of the Bride Speech Templates

SPEECH TEMPLATE 1

I'd like to welcome you all today to the wedding of my daughter [BRIDE] and her new husband [GROOM]. Thank you so much for sharing this special day with my dear wife [BRIDE'S MOTHER] and me.

You all probably noticed that my eyes watered just a bit during the ceremony; drat those pesky sinuses! (Pause for laughter) Oh, I might as well fess up, I was crying; this is truly an emotional day for me. The day that my dear, sweet daughter pledges her life to a great young man.

It seems like just yesterday I was holding my baby daughter in my arms, marveling at her incredible beauty and amazing sweetness. Now another man stares at her with loving, admiring eyes; and believe you me she's starin' right back (pause for laughter); my daughter is in love with her new husband, and I as a new papa could not be happier.

When you think about it, [BRIDE] and [GROOM] make the perfect couple. They're bright, sweet, attractive, successful, and are always the funniest ones at the dinner table. They're like a comedy duo that kisses from time to time; something that I'm really glad Martin and Lewis never did. (pause for laughter) As a matter of fact, I'd call these two a cross between Martin and Lewis and Rhett and Scarlett. The best of friends and lovers, these two really enjoy each other's company. I predict they'll have a great marriage.

Of course, I have seen them disagree from time to time; I raised my daughter to be strong and have her own opinions, and, furthermore, to express them. And believe you me, she EXPRESSES 'em. (pause for laughter) I encourage both her and my son-in-law to maintain their strong, independent spirits, while also learning the meaning of compromise. Talk things out, listen to one another, consider one another's needs, work together to solve your problems, and you'll be just fine.

Let me amend that; you won't be just fine. You'll be just fantastic. You two together make a beautiful, unbeatable team; a team sure to produce great children, impressive business and personal partnerships, and a lot of love. Not only the romantic love that exists between the two of you, but the divine love that surrounds you; that comes from the same friends and family members who came together today to honor your blessed union. These include my dear, sweet wife [MOTHER OF THE BRIDE], your dear friends [BRIDESMAIDS] and [GROOMSMEN], and [GROOM'S] wonderful parents, [MOTHER OF THE GROOM] and [FATHER OF THE GROOM]. It's been great getting to know your parents, [GROOM]; they're warm, bright, fantastic people who passed their many wonderful qualities onto you.

On this day, [GROOM], I'd like to welcome you officially to my family. You're a wonderful young man, and I've come to love you like a son. You treat my daughter like gold, and I can't tell you just how much I appreciate it. Keep it up, Kid; that is, after all, my little girl you just married. Treat her right. (grins almost evilly) Just a word of friendly advice from the man who helped pay for this wedding. Take it for what it's worth. (Pause for laughter).

And now a few words for that dear, precious daughter of mine. [BRIDE], I've watched you grow from an adorable little girl to a beautiful, sophisticated young woman. I've waited for this day for so long, and I can't wait to see what the future brings. As usual, you've made me proud today, by marrying a very special young man who I suspect will make a great husband. Take care of him, Kid; he loves you.

In the future, [GROOM] and [BRIDE], I wish you nothing but sweetness and bliss. Seize every day, savor every opportunity, dream plenty of dreams together. Then work hard to fulfill them. Together you two are unbeatable; together you can conquer the world.

Today, though, is just for having fun. Eat, drink, dance together, and dream of the future. Most of all, enjoy the company of those who love you. We do love you, [BRIDE] and [GROOM]. Congratulations, and please enjoy your wedding day.

SPEECH TEMPLATE 2

I'd like to welcome you all to the wedding of my daughter [BRIDE] and her husband [GROOM]. I'd have to say that my daughter's wedding day is the second happiest day of my life, and I thank you all for sharing it with me.

The happiest day of my life, of course, was the day I welcomed this beautiful creature into my life. From the first day I held my baby girl in my arms, I felt compelled to love, cherish and protect her. My daughter is my pearl; and I've always appreciated the fact that my wonderful, ravishing wife [MOTHER OF THE BRIDE] gave birth to my best friend. (To wife) Thanks a lot, Sweetie; I owe ya' one. (Pause for laughter)

Before my eyes, my precious, and though she won't admit it now somewhat precocious (pause for laughter) little girl has grown into a beautiful, intelligent, well-mannered, and sophisticated young woman. I was always proud of her, and was even more proud when she announced her engagement to a wonderful young man.

[GROOM] is, in many ways, [BRIDE'S] perfect mate. His wit, intelligence and success greatly impress me; and from what my daughter says, he's pretty darned hot to boot. (Pause for laughter) Always a bonus, I guess (shrugs, pauses for laughter). They make such a cute couple, and more importantly they listen to each other.

I am very confident that [BRIDE] and [GROOM] will have a beautiful future together; one filled with love and laughter, homes and trips, goals and dreams, and of course children. Hopefully a lot of 'em, if my wife gets her way. (Pauses for laughter)

As I get to know [FATHER OF THE GROOM] and [MOTHER OF THE GROOM], [GROOM'S] parents, I can see where he gets all of his stellar qualities. They're wonderful people and I want to issue them a warm welcome; not only to this wedding, but to my family.

And of course, I also want to send out this same warm welcome to my new son-in-law [GROOM]. You're a fine young man, one I consider my friend as well as a second son. And I'll say something else for you; you have great taste in women. (Pause for laughter)

[BRIDE], beyond being a good, loving daughter, you're just an amazing human being. I'm so proud of you— have I mentioned that yet today? (pause for laughter)— and I wish nothing but the best for you; not only in this marriage, but in life. Be happy, be healthy, be successful my girl; and never forget just how much your mother and I love you.

I sincerely hope that you're enjoying your wedding; not only the cake, the flowers and your beautiful dress, not only the devoted husband who obviously adores you, but the friends and family who have gathered here today to wish you well. Your dear friend

[BRIDESMAID], your husband's best buddy [GROOMSMAN], all your cousins, aunts, uncles and friends. These are the same people who will come to your aid in troubled times; who will be there for you through thick and thin.

Yep, Kid, I have to admit it; marriage is not always an easy road. You'll have your disagreements and outright arguments, your obstacles and temptations. You're only human beings, after all. (Pauses, smiles) But you're also great human beings. You're endlessly loving and respectful towards each other; each day you commit yourselves to taking care of each other. I'm very confident that you'll come through every challenge with flying, glowing colors. And you'll do it together, because you're so much in love.

In the future, I sincerely hope that you get everything you want and deserve. I just can't wait to see what the future holds; the beautiful homes, the successful business ventures, the many, many children (pauses), or maybe not so many. Don't faint on me dear. (Pause for laughter)

As always, my little girl, you hold the world in the palm of your dainty little hand. Have fun, embrace the future, and enjoy. I wish you and your new husband only the best of light, love, romance and happiness. We love you, Kids. Congratulations, and please enjoy your wedding day.

SPEECH TEMPLATE 3

I'd like to welcome you all to a very special day; the day that my baby girl gets married.

I think that most men approach this day with a mixture of unbridled joy and outright terror (pause for laughter). We take joy in knowing that our daughter is in love; that she's found the man of her dreams and heart, and that she's happy.

The terror part comes in when we realize that, well, that our daughter is in love (pause for laughter); that she's giving her heart to someone who could, potentially break her heart and severely impact her life.

I'm pleased to report, though, that I approach this day with nothing but sheer, unbridled joy. And for two reasons:

No. 1, my daughter [BRIDE] is a lady with a good head and strong values. She is independent—take it from her mom (MOTHER OF THE BRIDE) and me, who survived her teen years (pause for laughter)—and perfectly capable of making it on her own. My daughter will make a great wife, but she'll never be a submissive or clingy one. And, if the need arises, she'll make it just fine on her own.

Luckily, though, I don't think she'll ever face life on her own; this owing to the fact that my new son-in-law [GROOM] is a strong, dependable man who knows the meaning of the word commitment. He is a successful, educated man who takes his responsibilities very seriously. Most importantly, he loves my daughter beyond the point of reason. I strongly suspect that nothing, and no one, could drive these two apart.

Add to all that the fact that they're a drop dead cute couple who kiss and cuddle at every available opportunity (pause for laughter), and you've got what I call a winning couple.

Of course, I can definitely relate to all the kissing and cuddling stuff. My wife [MOTHER OF THE BRIDE] and I do both at every available opportunity; much to the chagrin and outright disgust of our children. (Pause for laughter) I also notice that [GROOM'S] parents, [GROOM'S MOTHER] and [GROOM'S FATHER], share this penchant for affection. They're a sweet, loving couple and I'm very happy to know them. And, needless to say, I'm very pleased to see them here today.

I'm also very pleased to see [GROOMSMEN] and [BRIDESMAID], trusted friends who have stood beside our kids during both challenging and happy days. This day definitely falls into that second category.

Together we've watched this beautiful couple as their romance has evolved, culminating in this day, a grand declaration of their love.

Grand, and may I add expensive. The money spent on her dress alone could feed most of the residents of any given third world country. (Pause for laughter) Ah, but it's all worth it; just look at how happy my girl is. (Smiles)

I just hope she and [GROOM] realize that marriage is not all about pretty dresses, handsome suits, fragrant flowers and fattening wedding cake. (Pause for laughter) Don't get me wrong, the cake was delicious, but it'll take me a flippin' month to work it off! (Pause for laughter)

What I really mean to say is, marriage isn't always about glamour and romance. (to the bride and groom) You two will see each other at your worst; I tell ya', you never grasp the true meaning of the term "in sickness and in health" until you see your wife nine months pregnant, or when she takes care of you during a nasty bout with the flu; holding the pail and everything. (Pause for laughter)

Ouch, I see [BRIDE] and [GROOM] running for the door. Maybe I got a little too real for them. (Pause for laughter) Come back and sit down, Kids, because I have some good news for you.

[GROOM], you'll think that [BRIDE] is equally beautiful in a maternity dress and a size eight wedding dress. And [BRIDE], you'll still think [GROOM] is a total hottie when he's leaning over that pail. (Pause for laughter) That's what love is all about; you grow to love a person's flaws as much as their assets. You'll cherish your partner in sickness and in health, for as long as you both shall live, all that jazz. (Pause for laughter)

{BRIDE] and [GROOM], we all love you and wish you the best for the future. Congratulations, you two; enjoy your wedding day.

SPEECH TEMPLATE 4

I'd like to welcome you all to the wedding of my daughter [BRIDE] and her new husband [GROOM]. I'm so pleased to share this truly beautiful day with all of you.

When a man has a daughter (though trust me, I never forget that it was my beautiful, amazing wife who actually gave birth to our precious girl—don't exile me to the couch tonight, Hon—pauses for laughter), he has a multitude of plans, dreams and aspirations for her.

He wonders if she'll be the next president, the next Miss America, the next Businesswoman of the Year, or maybe just a wife and mom who leads and loves a quiet life. Regardless of what she ultimately becomes, her father hopes that she'll find a man who nurtures and deserves her, and who loves her beyond the point of reason.

In [BRIDE], I'm so happy to say, I have the perfect daughter. She's bright and loving, intelligent and hard-working, charitable and thoughtful, successful and beautiful. And, also as per my dreams, she has found a guy that the kids today would deem "way cool." (Pauses) Those words sound absolutely ridiculous coming out of my mouth, don't they? (Pause for laughter) Moving right along now. (Pause for laughter)

[GROOM] is bright, handsome, kind and successful; he's the prince charming that a true princess like my daughter (not that I'm biased, of course—pause for laughter) deserves.

I foresee an ideal fairy tale future for the two of them, one that includes health, wealth, love and happiness. I can see the two of them embarking on a multitude of exciting adventures, but also taking some quiet time out to talk and enjoy their many common interests. I can see them having beautiful homes, great kids and fun trips. I can see them enjoying life, as well as each other.

I know that [GROOM'S] parents, [FATHER OF THE GROOM] and [MOTHER OF THE GROOM], share my great love for this young couple, and my intense enthusiasm for their future. They're great people and, as we've watched our children shape their future, I've really enjoyed getting the chance to know them and sharing this great happiness. I warmly welcome them to the family, along with their great son.

[GROOM] and [BRIDE], here's hoping that your future is a smooth and happy one. For those rare times when you do disagree, always remember that your family and friends are here to support you, just as we are today.

Your parents, your aunts and uncles, and those dear friends who stood beside you at the altar today will be there whenever you need help. Before you turn to them, though, always remember to turn first to each other. You're partners now; an unbeatable team.

Always remember to talk things out when you have problems, learn to make concessions for one another, and remember most of all the feelings of love and devotion that brought you here today. You two are very special people and an ideal couple.

And, lest you think I'm all mush and morals, as fathers sometimes are (pause for laughter), I also encourage you to have fun. Before you were mates and lovers you were great friends; never lose that sense of humor and enjoyment that has carried you this far.

Kiss, hug and laugh up a storm; even if some old codger occasionally tells you that you're too mushy to be believed. (Pause for laughter, then add sheepishly) This is just a hypothetical person, of course, no one you actually know. (Pause for laughter)

In closing, Kids, I just want to reassure you that the future is yours to enjoy. You're married now; the possibilities are as endless as your dreams. Stick together and you'll realize both. You two are incredible.

And speaking of incredible; [BRIDE], I still can't believe that you're all grown up and married now. I have news for you, though; as worldly and sophisticated as you've become, you're still and always my little girl.

I love you, Sweetheart. Many congratulations to you and your new husband, and may you both enjoy your wedding day—and your life together.

SPEECH TEMPLATE 5

I'd like to welcome you all to the wedding of my daughter [BRIDE] and her new husband [GROOM]. This is a beautiful day; one I'm honored to share with all of you.

As a father, I find that watching your child get married is a little like teaching her to ride a bike. You're so proud of her for taking this important step, but at the same time you're afraid she'll fall. So you watch with love and caution, you hold on for awhile, then you let go.

Today, sweet daughter, I'm letting go. I'm watching with pride as you embark on the adventure of a new life; a life with a very special young man.

Now please don't misunderstand. You know I'll always be there for you, ready with the love, compassion and of course money (pause for laughter) only a father can provide. Somehow, though, I don't think you'll need much help. You've chosen a young man who knows how to take care of you, just as you will care for him.

In the time I've spent with [GROOM], I've come to know him as a kind, sincere, intelligent young man; an ideal mate for my bright, beautiful daughter, and more importantly a solid helpmate.

He is always there when my daughter needs a friend, a shoulder to cry on, someone to kiss and compliment her. And she provides the same for him; they truly make an ideal couple. And I'm so pleased that my daughter has chosen this ideal man as her life mate.

I've also gotten to know [GROOM'S] parents, [GROOM'S MOTHER] and [GROOM'S FATHER], and find them to be just as bright, loving and witty as their son. I look forward to getting to know them better. They are already a part of our family.

And I also count our kids' attendants, [BRIDESMAID] and [GROOMSMAN] as part of the family. It's only fitting and symbolic that their best friends stand by them on this, the most beautiful day of their lives. Indeed, I appreciate greatly the presence of all the friends and family members here today; people here to celebrate and commemorate a very important day.

Important, and slightly nerve-wracking. All morning I've been pulling out what's left of my hair. (Pause for laughter) Still, I've noticed that [GROOM] and [BRIDE] have been miraculously calm and collected throughout this whole event; blast them! (Pause for laughter) Seriously though, this sense of calm and absolute reason will serve them well in their married life.

As will their capacity to kiss, endlessly and fervently. Did you catch that smooch at the altar? (Pause for laughter) These two are in love, it's easy to see; their love will realize and complete itself in the years to come, in the form of a beautiful home, many children, exciting adventures and mentally stimulating business ventures. Together these two are unbeatable.

Of course, as they ride this symbolic 'bicycle built for two' on the road to sickeningly sweet romance (pause for laughter), they're bound to hit a few bumps along the way. Even the best, happiest of couples face obstacles and temptations, have arguments and problems.

I have the feeling, though, that this couple will overcome all challenges with grace and love. They will deal with every situation by talking things out and reaching a compromise that's mutually agreeable to both of them. And they'll come out of these situations stronger and happier than ever.

Even in these difficult times, I truly have faith that this couple will make it. They seem very much like two halves of a radiant whole; two pieces of a beautiful puzzle. They are every silly romantic cliché you can think of (pause for laughter); although when you look at them together, you don't see 'silly,' you see 'amazing.'

In closing, [BRIDE] and [GROOM], I wish you nothing but the best in future years. I wish you love, laughter, light and romance. Seize the day, cherish every moment together, and go bravely—and hand into hand—into the future. Just remember to call home once in awhile! (Pause for laughter)

We love you so much, [BRIDE] and [GROOM]. Congratulations and enjoy the ride; for now, enjoy your wedding day.

SPEECH TEMPLATE 6

Good evening guests! It is my privileged as father of the bride to speak first at this occasion and steal all the attention from the rest of the speakers!

Those of you who know me will know that I don't really like public speaking, and that I often have little to say... but that is often due to all of the loud women in my life stealing my attention! That and on the subject of my daughter [DAUGHTER], I always have something to say!

I would like to start by welcoming you all today into our home to celebrate the marriage of [DAUGHTER] and [GROOM]. It has been such a fabulous day and it is really special to welcome you all here to party with this fabulous couple after such a beautiful service!

I know that so many of you have travelled many miles across land and ocean to be here today and on behalf of the newlyweds and their families, I'd like to take this moment to extend our deepest gratitude. I really do hope you have all enjoyed your day as it means so much to all of us to have you all here, without you it would be a very quiet party indeed!

I would also like to thank anyone and everyone who has had such a hand in creating this beautiful occasion. The friends and relatives who have donated so much time over the past three months to help us organize, choose decorations, cakes, food, dresses, make up, shoes... the list goes on... I'd thank you all personally but I'm not even sure how much actually went into this day, I just opened my wallet – my wife will thank you all and give you gifts of thanks after the speeches!

I know that many fathers give their potential sons-in-law real hell. But I'm just not that guy, besides, [GROOM] has become a real mate of mine over the years he has spent courting my daughter. He is an outstanding young man, and I'm very glad that I can still beat him at golf – though I'm guessing that won't last for much longer.

[GROOM] came into our lives a couple of years ago, attached to the arm of our eldest daughter .She was very goggle eyed over him, and he looked decidedly nervous. Poor thing. I love my daughter but she is quite a handful!

[DAUGHTER] has always been a lovely young woman, when she was a baby she used to throw food at me, when she was a little girl she thought I was the best thing in the world, and then as a teenager she used to throw anything she could get her hands on at me. And I've always loved her, every minute, every tantrum, every tear and every fit of hysterical laughter that has rolled out of her.

My first child, and my most challenging, it is with a lot of emotion and tears that I gave her away today. There were times that she used to ask me to give her away when she was an outlandish teen; she really was quite funny – though if you laughed at her, she'd throw more things at you. Her hair was always an outrageous color and she drove her mother up the wall.

And then there would be moments when she would come and curl up on the couch next to me and let me give her a bit of a cuddle.

Then she hit college and she straightened right out. She studied hard, she'd done all of her rebelling, and she's turned into a fine young woman with a heart of gold and the loyalty of a lion.

[DAUGHTER], I am so proud of you, I have always loved you and you look so beautiful today. You are a one in a million and I know that you will take your new husband on an incredible adventure through life, and I really do wish for you every happiness in the world.

On that note, if we would please all charge our glasses and raise them in a toast to the bride and groom.

To [DAUGHTER] and [GROOM] may you laugh together, love together and always be together.

Congratulations!

SPEECH TEMPLATE 7

Here I am! I know this is the moment of the day you have all been waiting for – all of you on the edge of your seat waiting for me to impart my pearls of wisdom.

Well, I'm terribly sorry to disappoint.

I was going to start my speech today using the formal address of ladies and gentlemen... but then when I look around the room I see all of these adult versions of the kids I used to know. Not only my own kids, but my nieces and nephews, the kid's friends... and then there are all these geriatrics – my friends and my siblings... I guess we are all getting older.

Today is one of the happiest days of my life; I am without a doubt the proudest man in the world. Today I watched my daughter [DAUGHTER] marry her prince charming. There is nothing better for any father than to see your little girl looking so happy and so beautiful on the day of her wedding. It was a little emotional for me and [WIFE], giving away our little girl – I'm not big on sharing, but I know she will be in good hands – and so, I tried to be generous.

For this I really want to thank [GROOM's] parents [NAMES]. They have done a wonderful job in raising this bright, intelligent and mature young man. It has been great knowing you guys and my wife [NAME] and I look forward to spending more quality time with you.

When [DAUGHTER] was born I was a nervous wreck, but I was instantly calmed the moment I held that little baby. She didn't cry, she didn't fuss, she was an incredible baby who turned into a very happy and outgoing (some say precocious – but I was told to be nice!) little girl. She was always clever – sometimes outsmarted her parents – and she always had a wonderful sense of humor.

[DAUGHTER] always kept her mother and me on our toes. A bit of a wild child, she was a diehard party animal that we couldn't contain. But she was always lovely at home, her room was cleaned when she was told and she was charming and kind and loving to her younger siblings... We just adored her – we have always been proud of you sweet heart – and despite your constant rebelling against our parenting – we think you have turned into a pretty fantastic young woman – with or without our help!

Most parents have trouble getting through to their kids, and we weren't any different. Our gorgeous daughter didn't listen to our advice. But I hope she will today. I've been married for almost thirty years and so I think I'm just as qualified as anyone to give advice on marriage... so listen up [DAUGHTER] this one is for you!

Marriage is an adventure and success is not automatic. Like most things in life, as you have learnt, you have to work at it. Sometimes you will be annoyed, sometimes you will even find each other maddening. Get over it.

Life is hard sometimes, and what you have in each other is something worth working for. You will learn skills that you can (attempt to) pass on to your children.

You will learn patience, tolerance and acceptance. Together you will share the happiest moments in your life, and the saddest. You will need to put the other person first. Marriage is not just about finding the perfect partner – which is step one – the rest of it is doing everything you can to BE the perfect partner.

There is nothing better than seeing your eyes sparkle with so much love, and I hope that you will hold onto that love and treat it with the respect and care that it deserves.

Now, [GROOM], there are three phrases that I have learnt are the key to you being a successful husband... use them appropriately! The first is 'YES DEAR' – use those three words as often as you like. In an argument this one works a charm, 'of course it's me that is wrong, I'm sorry.' And finally perhaps the most important, 'no, your bum does not look big in that!'

I am so proud of you both, it has been a beautiful day, an incredible ceremony and a delicious dinner, and with all of these friends and family around you to celebrate your love – there couldn't be a more perfect way to start off a life of wedded bliss.

On that note, I would like to propose a toast. So please charge your glasses and be upstanding.

To [DAUGHTER] and [GROOM] may your marriage be long and fruitful, full of laughter and love, we love you, congratulations!

SPEECH TEMPLATE 8

Good afternoon everyone, for those of you that don't know me, I am [NAME], the proud father of the pride and I am here to speak to you on behalf of my family, our kids and my wife, [WIFE], the equally excited and proud mother of the bride!

[WIFE] and I would sincerely like to welcome you all here today to celebrate the love and joy that we feel at the union of our beautiful daughter [DAUGHTER] and her handsome new husband [GROOM].

I know that many of you have travelled from far and wide to be here with us today, and I would like to thank you all for your effort. It means so much to all of us to have so many friends and family here today in total support for this wonderful young couple and to truly give them the happiest start to their wedded life possible!

I would also like to take this opportunity to thank [GROOMS PARENTS], who are [GROOM]'s mom and dad and have been a never ending fountain of love and support for our daughter and who have done so much to help [WIFE] and I make today possible. I know that all four of us are overwhelmed and full of so much love for the new bride and groom, and we will all probably be a little bit of an emotional wreck for the rest of the night.

Thank you to you both for being such wonderful parents, for raising such a good man and for being such fabulous second parents to our daughter. We know how much she loves you and it really is special to know that she has another safe place to go for love and support.

I couldn't have imagined a better partner for my beautiful daughter. [GROOM] is a very special young man. He has brought so much happiness into our home and always comes with a good joke and his cooking skills have never gone to waste! I know that he will be a wonderful husband to our daughter and will care for her and love her and respect her in the way that she deserves.

When my little girl was born, 28 years ago, I was just a young man with a full head of hair and much less of a belly... and now here we are. When I held that tiny baby, I couldn't imagine her fully grown, I couldn't imagine ever finding anyone I'd be happy to give her away to. Until today.

When I gave away [DAUGHTER] today, I knew that she was going into the care of someone who would do anything for her and give her anything she ever needs. And that is something truly wonderful for any father.

There is nothing better in the world than seeing your child go into a union with someone that they love and respect and care for... And someone that can put up with their outlandish behavior! It isn't easy to give away your daughter, or to finally realize that you are getting old, but I couldn't imagine a more beautiful day to do both of those things...

My last wedding speech was nearly 30 years ago, at my own wedding, and I was so nervous, and so in love with my new wife [WIFE], and boy, hasn't it been an adventure. Three kids and years of laughter and tears and stress and joy – and here we are, not quite as tight or well groomed as we were back then, but happier than ever.

For you, [DAUGHTER] and [GROOM] I want the life that I have been lucky to have. I want for you the beautiful marriage, the wonderful children, the happy days and the support and the years of love and the wonderful memories.

I know I am supposed to tell some embarrassing stories about my beautiful daughter, but she has threatened my life if I dare – and I'd have to admit that she would have much better stories about me, granted I have had many more years to make a fool out of myself. So I think I'll leave it there...

[DAUGHTER], I've only ever wanted the best for you I want you to have all the happiness in the world, and I think you have got that today. I love you and I hope that your future is as bright and happy as your past and your love is never ending.

On that note, I'd like you to all raise your glasses and toast the newlyweds and their happiness.

To [DAUGHTER] and [GROOM], may you live long and happily in each other's arms.

Congratulations sweetheart.

SPEECH TEMPLATE 9

Good evening to you all. Family and friends new and old, it is my absolute honor to stand in front of you today as father of the bride, and what a beautiful bride!

Before I really get into this speech – I'd just like to ask you please not to stand on any of the chairs or tables during my standing ovation – it breaches all kinds of health and safety regulations.

Seriously though, I was strictly told to keep this short by my darling daughter [DAUGHTER], so I trimmed it down and now it is only 30 minutes. So get comfortable, you're in for a long ride.

I'd like to first start by thanking each and every one of you for joining us in the celebration of [DAUGHTER] and [GROOM]'s wedding and the love that they share for each other. I was going to thank each and every one of you individually, but due to the evil stares of my darling wife, I think I should cut that bit out... making my speech only a few more minutes long...

Weddings are so much fun; they are an excuse for a great big party and today is certainly no exception. We have so many wonderful people here with us today, both of the newlywed's extended families, grandparents, step parents, children and friends who are all here to truly celebrate this joyous union in style!

So, thank you all for being here, it wouldn't be such a party without you! And to [GROOM]s parents [GROOMS PARENTS], thank you so much for all of your help with today, your constant involvement and support for this great couple and can I just tell you now on behalf of my wife [WIFE] and I, how glad we are to have you in our lives and in the life of our precious daughter.

She loves you very much and your support and kindness towards her has brought her so much joy, and thus, you have brought us a lot of joy! We really do look forward to joining our families together to celebrate the holidays!

I haven't given a speech since my own wedding – which was about 30 years ago... I was so nervous. Full of jitters, and full of love, and I'm sure that is how [BRIDE] and [GROOM] are feeling today.

There is something really magical about a wedding, about seeing a young couple join together in the church they were both baptized in, and really profess their love together in the eyes of god and all of their friends and family.

For me, as the father of the bride, there has never been a moment more proud or a moment more tinged with sadness. [DAUGHTER] getting married today means that she is no longer mine – in fact, I even went through the ritual of giving her away – much to my own dismay.

But I will say this, that although my little girl is no longer mine, will no longer live under my roof, will no longer make me coffee on a Sunday morning, will no longer pick me up from the pub on a Friday night... I will love her all the same.

And if I had to give my daughter away to anyone, [GROOM] would be the man. So thankfully it has all turned out for the best!

[DAUGHTER] has always been my little princess, the youngest of four boys, the little girl, the crowning glory – and I'll admit it now, I spoiled her... but who wouldn't! And I know that [GROOM] will continue to give her everything she could possibly need...

[GROOM] is a good man, from a good family and I know that he will care for my daughter and come over and watch football with me and that sometimes he might even drive me home from the pub!

It's a good life, and life is for living, so the only advice I have for you two love birds today, is to live your life! Get out there and go on adventures, see the world, do whatever is in your heart because you only get one shot at it, and you get it together – so get out there and really live! We will support you every step of the way!

On that note, I'd like to propose a toast to the bride and groom; if you would all join me and be upstanding.

To [DAUGHTER] and [GROOM] may your house always be filled with laughter, wine and great food – and may you never forget to visit your parents!

Congratulations.

SPEECH TEMPLATE 10

Ladies and gentlemen, on behalf of [DAUGHTER] and [GROOM] it is my absolute pleasure to extend a warm welcome to you all to this their wedding reception.

I want to keep my speech short, as I have the honor of going first there are a lot of other people itching to get up here and put their two cents in... That and [DAUGHTER] threatened me with my life to keep the speech above board and not embarrass her too much!

First of all I would like to congratulate my beautiful daughter and her handsome new husband on the first day of many together as man and wife. It is a wonderful adventure that you have embarked on together today and it truly is wonderful to see so many people who have come out to support them and celebrate their love.

It has been a beautiful ceremony and a truly delightful dinner, and I'd like to take this opportunity to thank everyone who has been involved in helping us make this day happen. The ladies with the dresses, the cake, the caterer, the vicar, the ushers and all of the friends and family who pitched in to help out – thank you! We just couldn't have done it without you!

It fills me with pride to see my youngest child, my little girl, [DAUGHTER], with such happiness in her eyes and in her heart. I honestly believe that she has found someone to keep her happy forever.

[DAUGHTER] was a mischievous little girl, she used to take trinkets from her mother and her older siblings and create weddings in our backyard. She was always the bride, and who she married depended on how patient the dog, cat, bird or teddy bear were feeling at any given time .I'm glad that [GROOM] didn't have to be collared and leashed today, but came along willingly!

[DAUGHTER] has always brought me so much joy and has brought a lot of laughter and love into our hearts and home since the day we knew she existed.

She has always been our baby, and now we see our baby is all grown, and with all that happiness comes a little sadness for us, [WIFE] and myself, her parents. But with that sadness also comes a realization that we are now free to do what we want!

Our kids are all grown up and with our youngest embarking on the happiest relationship with her heart full of love and her mind full of hope and expectation – nothing could make us happier.

Now as for the choice of groom! I have to say that [GROOM] is a very welcome new member of our family, he has always been much loved at our house and very welcome, especially around the holidays when he truly shines.

[GROOM] came into our lives over a nervous dinner a couple of years ago and we haven't been able to get rid of him since. It has always been obvious how much he loves [DAUGHTER] and so he's always been alright by me.

But over the years he has become more than just my kid's boyfriend, but he has become a friend of mine as well. There is always a place on the couch for him on sports day and he has charmed my wife within an inch of her life. The girls are always fawning over him and he always pretends he hates it – even though I'm sure it's the opposite.

[GROOM] is a great man, and I think that is much due to his wonderful parents [GROOMS PARENTS] and their excellent parenting. Thank you both for raising such a man for our daughter, they truly are perfect for each other.

I have all of the faith in the world that this couple is indeed perfect and that they will take very good care of each other every day for the rest of their lives. And one day their family will grow and they will understand this love and pride and joy that parents feel...

On that note, will you please all join me in a toast to the happy couple?

Please raise your glasses and be upstanding.

To [BRIDE] and [GROOM] the bride and groom, may your future be bright and happy, may you always be brave and remember your love for each other throughout your adventure of life, may you always laugh together and cry together.

Congratulations – you are both very loved.

Crafting your Speech

This section will help you to craft your own speech and come up with something that will surely leave you with a smile of achievement.

Clarity of Mind

Before you sit down to actually write your speech you need to make a few things clear in your mind:

1. What is the purpose of giving a speech – obviously the reason is that you are the father of the bride and want to express your love and good wishes for your daughter and future son-in-law?

2. What message do you want to give out to the family of son-in-law, son-in-law, your daughter and the family and friends present?

3. How do you want the guests to feel after you have delivered your speech?

Getting the Facts Right

1. Before writing the speech please make sure that you remember the names of all the important people involved in the wedding like the names of the groom's parents, the names of any of bride's friends that you will be mentioning in your

speech, the names of Best Man, Maid of Honor or any others that you will be talking about in your speech

2. If you are saying a story or an anecdote please ensure that you remember the time when the story took place (how old your daughter was at that time), the time when the bride and the groom first met, names of people involved in that story or incident. This will make it sound realistic and will make it interesting

3. Remember the things in which the bride excelled, the things that she dislikes, any interesting story about her growing up years, facts about her courtship with the groom. Make them a part of your speech

4. Have a casual chat with your daughter and other important people involved so that things are crystal clear in your mind before you begin to make it a part of your speech

5. You will come across more incidents and funny stories when you talk to the bride's friends and close people, the groom and others. There may be incidents that you may have forgotten. These can be included in your speech. As you talk to people you will get more and more ideas.

6. Just keep writing small, little notes as you come across information. These notes can be converted into an excellent speech

7. Asking some of the following questions will give you more ideas for your speech:

   - How did the groom and the bride first meet?

   - Where did they meet?

   - When did they meet?

   - Was anyone responsible for bringing them together?

   - How did the groom propose the bride or vice versa?

   - When and where was the proposal made?

   - What was the reaction of the proposal?

   - Has anything funny happened during their courtship?

   - What is that one thing that the bride loves about the groom and vice versa?

   - What are the individual goals of the bride and the groom and what are their goals as a married couple?

8. Now you have so much of information to pick and choose from. You have come across so many new things that you did not know about.

9. Walking down the memory lane will give you more ideas about the funny things or lovely things that your daughter did while she was growing up

10. It is also a good idea to have a little bit of idea about the kind of guests that will be attending the wedding. Their average age group, their religious believes, what kind of stuff will be accepted as funny. A look at the guest list will give you a rough idea

Organizing your Thoughts

Before you begin to write you must decide the basic content of your speech. Whether you plan to quote several small little incidents related to your daughter's life or you plan to narrate one story throughout the speech.

It is very important to decide upon a theme for your speech. Either you touch upon 2-3 small incidents related to the same theme or focus on building upon just one story related to that theme. Do not go overboard with mentioning too many incidents or getting into too many details. This will confuse and bore your audience.

Making the First Draft

While writing a rough sketch of your speech just keep deleting the incidents that you feel are not so worth mentioning. Every memory with your daughter is special and there may be many incidents or stories that you may want to share. But you must remember that you have to pick and choose only the important ones. Talking about too many stories will make your speech a drab.

In a five to seven minute speech you only have enough time to cover two or three points MAXIMUM!

Now that you have selected 2-3 good stories or even decided to focus on one single story, your speech is already gaining a clean and organized structure.

Remember you must always choose stories/incidents that will evoke a reaction among your audience. It could be either an emotional reaction or people might find something funny and laugh. The idea is to strike the right chord with your audience and stir their hearts.

Keep your stories short and crisp but please ensure that your audience completely understands what you are trying to say. To be able to connect to your speech they should be able to completely understand the details and the punch behind that story. In those short few lines you should be able to convey the story and the audience should also be clear as to why you have included it in your speech.

Just keep writing brief notes of whatever you want to include in your speech. Don't worry about the length of the speech at this stage. You can always edit it later on. Right now the important thing is to have all your thoughts on paper and in one place.

Use simple words. Even if you have Shakespeare's vocabulary please do not use fancy, complicated words as your audience might not be able to relate to these words. Keep it simple and easy to understand.

Avoid repetition at all costs.

A good speech has three parts the opening, the body and the conclusion.

1. Your opening remarks should capture the audience attention
2. The body of your speech should support your opening remarks
3. The conclusion should reinforce the opening and your body in a
memorable heartfelt way.

Now that you have got all your thoughts as points on paper you need to organize them and put them in the above structure. Good speech organization is essential if the audience is to follow your speech.

Do not worry about perfection at this stage. Just think about beginning to write. Once you get into the flow of writing other things can be fixed later on.

Do not worry about gaining audience attention as it is quite easy to get audience pay attention to you in case of a Wedding Speech. The reason being that the theme of the speech is love and relationship and people are quite keen to know interesting stories about both the bride and the groom.

While writing your draft remember to stick to the theme of your speech about the couple, their courtship, your relationship with them, their bright future together. Do not deviate from the main theme.

The Opening

The first thing to remember in the opening of the speech is that you must sound enthusiastic and involved. You might be tired but don't show it. The opening of your speech sets the mood of your entire speech.

Create an interesting opening that captures the audience's attention.

It is often better to say a quick witty joke, or one liner to grab the audience attention, making sure not to offend anyone.

In the beginning always introduce yourself. The bride is an integral part of the occasion, a very important part that should be referenced somewhere in the opening remarks of your speech.

It is always a good idea to try and memorize the beginning 2- 3 lines of your speech.

Remember that your audience actually wants to hear what you have to say.

The impact of standing up, lifting your head and speaking to the audience will help make them feel immediately part of the wedding speech.

If humor is not your cup of tea and you are uncomfortable being funny please do not attempt to be funny. It's perfectly all right to stick to your own style and be warm and gentle.

If you are extremely nervous it is always good to admit it. A line in the beginning like "Hello my name is .... I am the bride's father and I am extremely nervous." This is an excellent icebreaker line and will also evoke humor.

The Body (Middle)

The best way to lay out the body of your speech is by formulating a series of points that you would like to raise. The points should be organized so that related points follow one another and each point builds upon the previous one. This will also give your speech a more logical progression.

You will only have time to cover two or three points maximum, so keep your stories small and straight to the point. Don't get caught up on the detail of your stories.

Make the body of the speech a sequence of little build-ups to a climax or punch line.

The trick is to try and keep momentum going with your speech. So do break down your body into one or two stories, and never deliver a monologue of past events as this will bore your audience to death.

Make your speech emotional and get your audience involved in the speech. Apply the **think, feel, act** formula. Share a story that leads them to **think**, then show how emotional you are today, this will make them **feel** and finally request them to join you in wishing the couple the best, thus they **act**.

Choose your stories in such a way that you can have the audience engaged in these stories and they can relate to these stories on a personal level. A few lines on the bride's first meeting with the groom's parents and how impressed she was to meet them, will not only involve the groom's parents but will also involve your audience as they will think that you will share more stories with them during the speech.

It is also a good idea to throw in a marriage or love quotation but make sure you do not use too many quotations in your speech and that the quotations you choose are very relevant and appropriate. (Refer to the section that offers lots of love and wedding quotations and toasts).

The Conclusion

Experts say that in the opening and closing of the speech you must remember to re-emphasize the theme of your speech.

You must restate and not REPEAT the main points in the closure of the speech. Just summarize one or two most important points of your speech in the conclusion. For example if the bride and the groom met each other in a dance school and you have mentioned it in the body of your speech, you can end by saying, "Jane and Tim, look where your dancing has got you to. Hope you dance as perfect partners throughout your life."

End by offering a toast to bride and the groom. You should however have two or three different toasts ready to call upon as it is possible that someone else has already used your toast. (Refer to the section that offers lots of love and wedding quotations and toasts).

Fine Tuning

Once you have completed your draft it is time to read it several times, edit and delete the unimportant portions and polish it up

Take a stop watch, read out the speech and time it. This will give you the duration of your speech which is a very critical aspect of speech giving

It is always a good idea to take a second opinion on your speech from your spouse, your friend or anyone who you feel might be able to give you an unbiased view

Now that your speech is ready, it is always good to practice it several times. Reading it loud and clear. Sometimes in front of someone or sometimes even in front of a mirror. Emphasize on the main points. Use eye contact, facial expressions, gestures. (Refer to the section that offers tips and tricks on delivering a speech). Practicing several times will boost your confidence level and will give you the command over your speech. The more number of times you rehearse the better you will get. It's simple.

Most professional speakers use cue cards to deliver a seamless speech. Write the important points of your speech on the cue card and use it as a reference while giving the speech on the final day. It is perfectly all right if the audience comes to know that you are using cue cards. You can't be expected to memorize the entire speech. In case if a sudden mental block occurs, the cue card will come to your rescue.

Closing Remarks

Hope this section has helped you to get an overview of how to craft a speech that will hold the attention of your audience, will impress the newlywed couple and will be remembered for a long long time to come.

The speech samples provided in this book will give you a better idea about how to write a great speech and not just a good speech. You can in fact pick and choose portions from these sample speeches and make them a part of your own speech. The samples are written in such a manner that they can be easily adapted to your situation and can be easily used after making minor changes.

Overcoming Public Speaking Fears

I realize when it comes to speech giving both content as well as presentation is equally important. Even if your content is brilliant but if you do not know how to speak your speech well with confidence, things will fall flat. The art of speech giving is a combination of the matter of the speech as well as confident delivery of it.

In this section you will learn the tips on how to overcome public speaking fears and make your speech picture perfect.

12 things to remember before you take on the stage

Practice leads to perfection – Even if your speech is 4-5 minutes long it is always recommended to practice before taking on the stage. Practicing in front of a mirror always helps. Even though it sounds funny but BELIEVE ME IT HELPS!! It gives you an idea about your facial expressions, hand movements and body language and gestures. You can immediately catch hold of and get rid of something that looks awkward. Something that you may have easily missed because of not having a mirror.

Use cue cards – Even if your memory is very good it is always a good idea to carry cue cards/index cards. Do not write the entire speech and read it out. This will never give a good impression. Writing small points in the cue cards and using it as a reference will always help. You can always glance through these cue cards while giving out the speech. Please ensure you number your cards so there is no confusion.

Avoid long speeches – A long speech is considered drab and boring. Make sure you edit you speech before taking on the stage. Everyone is interested in quick and interesting stories not in lectures! Keep your speech 5-7 minutes long. It is always good to time your speech with a stop watch beforehand.

Avoid unwanted humor – Please do not quote stories of ex relationships of the bride and the groom. This will unnecessarily embarrass them and will not give out a positive impression about you.

Eye Contact - Establishing eye contact with your audience is very important. Look around the room at guests smiling. This will show the audience you are confident. It will surely make you feel in command of the situation.

Speed of the speech – Do not rush through as it will give the impression that you want to just get over with it. Take pauses. Relax! Give emphasis. It will show your confidence. If you rush too much audience will lose the important parts of your speech. Remember you have practised your speech many times but the audience is hearing it for the first time.

Take your audience with you - Let the audience grasp what you are saying. Slow paced speech will ensure that the audience is following what you are saying. Make sure you are not too slow also otherwise people might get bored. The trick is to be involved with what you are saying rather than just reading out what you have prepared.

Support your speech with small anecdotes and examples - If you include funny incidents in your speech it will not only make your speech interesting but will also retain the audience attention. Where you expect the audience to laugh just pause and let them enjoy the moment. Rushing too much will spoil the fun of the moment.

Be involved – Just be involved with what you are saying. This will make your speech natural and free flowing. If the audience makes a positive comment, while you are giving the speech, acknowledge it. This will engage the audience and make them feel important.

Take Pride – It is indeed an honor to be requested by the groom and the bride to give a speech. Take pride in the fact and speak from your heart. If you talk from heart you can't go wrong.

Avoid alcohol – Avoid too much alcohol at any cost. Please hold back on alcohol till you have given out your speech. Alcohol will not only distract you from what you have prepared but will also prevent you from being at your best.

Finally, Smile – Smiling will not only make you feel confident but will also hold the interest of the audience giving out positive energy and vibes and making them feel welcomed.

Making it Picture Perfect

To make sure your speech is the most memorable and entertaining speech of the day, content as well as presentation is equally important. For presenting a speech the crucial aspects you should take care of are:

Voice Modulations

- Make sure your voice is loud and clear (audible even to the last person in the hall). Ensure that your mouth is in synch with the placement of the microphone. You will have to adjust your voice pitch with that of the microphone. Too loud a voice will sound shrilling on the microphone. Don't get too hassled with it. You will naturally understand it within the first 30 seconds as you begin to talk

- If there is some trouble with the microphone DO NOT PANICK. This is normal. Just try to make sure the microphone is switched on and if you can't fix the problem yourself look around for help. There will surely be help at hand

- Avoid pronouncing words you are not comfortable with.

- Take a deep breath before beginning and tell your mind to 'RELAX'. This will avoid the shakiness in your voice and make your voice sound confident

- Be enthusiastic about your speech. This will make your voice sound full of positive energy and confidence

- Pause at the important points to ensure what you are saying sinks well with the audience

- Emphasize on important words. This will ensure that audience attention is retained

- Do not be in a rush to finish the speech. Speak slowly and surely

- It's perfectly all right if you flutter a bit. Just continue and move on to the next point

Body Language

- Stand straight/erect smartly with equal weight on both the legs

- Release all your body tension

- Maintain eye-contact with your audience while talking. This will keep them engaged

- Do not just look towards one side of the room on a particular set of audience. Make sure you establish eye-contact with the entire audience

- Give a glance to the bride and the groom when you are mentioning an incident or story about them

- Keep glancing at the cue cards every once in a while. Pick up a point and talk to the audience. After a little while glance again at the cue cards and pick up another point

Facial Expressions

- Smile at the beginning and also in between the speech as and when the script of your speech demands

- Look confident and straight

- Just be yourself. Do not try to imitate or try to be someone else

Hand Gestures

- Do not put your hands in front or at your back for too long a time

- Use your hands sometimes to emphasize a point

- Avoid constant fidgeting with your hands

Oooops those nerve-wrecking moments!!!

Always remember you are not the only one who has public speaking fears. It's perfectly ALL RIGHT to be a little nervous.

To break the ice, you can always admit your nervousness to the audience and smile. In that case even if you make a mistake people will have empathy and will not mind that much. Don't think that if you flutter or make a mistake people will laugh at you. Not at all. Everyone understands that it takes courage to go up there and talk.

Practice well in advance. Even though it might appear useless beforehand but it will always help you when you are in front of a room full of people.

Tell your mind to 'RELAX'. This will relax your nerves and make you feel confident.

Enjoy the moment.

When you are invited on the stage to give your speech walk briskly with full confidence and approach the dais/podium. Establish eye-contact with the audience, smile briefly, take pride in your speech, take a deep breath and begin with the speech. This will give the impression that you are in command of the situation.

Have confidence in yourself and all that you have learned from this book and practised. If you just follow it and trust yourself nothing can go wrong.

Last but not the least the trick of delivering a good speech is just be yourself!

Love and Wedding Quotations

A wedding speech is incomplete without some relevant and heartwarming quotations thrown in here and there. These quotations will not only continue to hold the attention of the guests but will also make your speech memorable and outstanding.

Here are a whole lot of very exclusive quotations. Go ahead and take your pick!

Amy Bloom

Love at first sight is easy to understand; it's when two people have been looking at each other for a lifetime that it becomes a miracle.

Ann Landers

All married couples should learn the art of battle as they should learn the art of making love. Good battle is objective and honest--never vicious or cruel. Good battle is healthy and constructive, and brings to a marriage the principle of equal partnership.

Georg C. Lichtenberg

Love is blind, but marriage restores its sight.

Homer

There is nothing nobler or more admirable than when two people who see eye to eye keep house as man and wife, confounding their enemies and delighting their friends.

Elbert Hubbard

Love grows by giving. The love we give away is the only love we keep. The only way to retain love is to give it away.

Joseph Barth

Marriage is our last, best chance to grow up.

Louis K. Anspacher

Marriage is that relation between man and woman in which the independence is equal, the dependence mutual, and the obligation reciprocal.

Pearl S. Buck

A good marriage is one which allows for change and growth in the individuals and in the way they express their love.

Robert C. Dodds

The goal in marriage is not to think alike, but to think together.

Simone Signoret

Chains do not hold a marriage together. It is threads, hundreds of tiny threads which sew people together through the years.

Tom Mullen

Happy marriages begin when we marry the ones we love, and they blossom when we love the ones we marry.

George Elliott (aka Mary Anne Evans), Adam Bede

What greater thing is there for two human souls than to feel that they are joined for life - to strengthen each other in all labor, to rest on each other in all sorrow, to minister to each other in all pain, to be one with each other in silent, unspeakable memories at the moment of the last parting.

Sam Keen

You come to love not by finding the perfect person, but by seeing an imperfect person perfectly.

Louis Ginsberg

Love is the irresistible desire to be desired irresistibly.

Elizabeth Thomas

Love and commitment are rocks. Don't let the running waters move your marriage rock.

Harville Hendrix

Marriage, ultimately, is the practice of becoming passionate friends.

Oscar Wilde

Ultimately the bond of all companionship, whether in marriage or in friendship,
is conversation.

Cokie Roberts

There is such pleasure in long-term marriage that I really would hate to be
my age and not have had a long-term marriage.
Remember, sustaining a pleasurable, long-term
marriage takes effort, deliberateness and an intention to learn about one another.

Jon BonJovi

As for his secret to staying married: "My wife tells me that if I ever
decide to leave, she is coming with me."

Cicero

The First Bond of Society is Marriage.

Nathaniel Hawthorne

What a happy and holy fashion it is that those who love one another should rest on the same pillow.

Peter De Vries

The bonds of matrimony are like any other bonds - they mature slowly.

Maxwell Anderson

If two stand shoulder to shoulder against the gods,
Happy together, the gods themselves are helpless
Against them while they stand so.

George Levinger

What counts in making a happy marriage is not so much how compatible you are, but how you deal with incompatibility.

William Lyon Phelps

The highest happiness on earth is marriage.

Oliver Wendell Holmes

Love is the master key that opens the gates of happiness.

Toni Sciarra Poynter

You don't need to be on the same wavelength to succeed in marriage. You just need to be able to ride each other's waves.

Ellen Goodman

We are told that people stay in love because of chemistry, or because they remain intrigued with each other, because of many kindnesses, because of luck. But part of it has got to be forgiveness and gratefulness.

Andre Maurois

A successful marriage is an edifice that must be rebuilt every day.

Andre Maurois

A happy marriage is a long conversation which always seems too short.

Helen Keller

The best and most beautiful things in the world cannot be seen or even touched. They must be felt with the heart.

Some more Quotations for you that can be placed on Menu Cards and Place Cards

Love one another ..and you will be happy.
It's as simple... .. and as difficult as that.

Two souls with but a single thought,
Two hearts that beat as one.

I will not love you for the rest of your life,
but for the rest of mine

This day I will marry my friend,
the one I laugh with, live for, dream with, love.

Knowing you'll be in all my tomorrows,
makes my today so wonderful

We may not have it all together, but together we have it all.

You two have decided that
You'll share one house for life,
And call yourselves, instead of friends,

A husband and a wife.

3 cups Love
2 cups Warmth
1 cup Forgiveness
1 cup Friends
4 spoon Hope
2 spoons Tenderness
1 pint Faith
1 barrel Laughter

Combine love & warmth
Mix thoroughly with tenderness
Add forgiveness
Blend with friends & hope
Sprinkle all remaining tenderness
Stir in faith and laughter
Bake with sunshine
Serve daily in generous helpings.

Henceforth there shall be such a oneness between you,
that when one weeps, the other will taste salt.

How beautiful life can be when touched by love.
It doesn't matter where you go in life, or what you do,
or how much you have, it's who you have beside you.

Of all the joys of a long happy life,
there's none so precious as the love
between husband and wife.

Together is a wonderful place to be.

Two hearts once joined in friendship, united now with love.

Dance through life with me - the best is yet to be.

From long ago and far away
love brought us to our wedding day!

Some things are simply meant to be, like finding your soul mate, your heart's destiny.

The beginning of a beautiful forever!

The joining of two hands makes one heart!

Let our love be like an arch - two weaknesses learning together to form one strength.

Life is a journey, and I'm so glad we're traveling together!

Life's hard journey can be endured if we travel hand in hand.

Two hearts, two minds, two lives - one never-ending love.

What greater thing is there for two human souls than to

feel
that they are joined for life.

What's the earth with all its art, verse, music worth - compared with love, found, gained, and kept?

When two hearts unite, the road is short, the burden is light.

Marriage is choosing someone again and again to love and to cherish with each new dawn.

Marriage is friendship's highest ideal.

Marriage is love personified.

Seek not every quality in one individual

More marriages might survive if the partners realized that sometimes the better comes after the worst.

Love is moral even without legal marriage, but marriage is immoral without love.

Marriage should be a duet- when one sings, the other claps

She who has never lov'd, has never liv'd.

A successful marriage requires falling in love many times, always with the same person.

Never go to bed mad. Stay up and fight.

Getting married is easy. Staying married is more difficult. Staying happily married for a lifetime should be ranked among the fine arts.

In marriage, being the right person is as important as finding the right person.

Where there is great love, there are always miracles.

Then I saw you through myself and found we were identical.

Love is determined not for time you spend telling each other I love you. It is the value of the love shared by two as one.

Love is that condition in which the happiness of another person is essential to your own.

Funny Wedding Quotations

Here are a few funny wedding quotations and one-liners to bring a smile on the guest's faces and to make your speech interesting and appealing.

Helen Rowland

In olden times sacrifices were made at the altar -- a practice which is still continued.

Anonymous

Marriages are made in heaven. But, again, so are thunder, lightning, tornados and hail.

Ambrose Bierce

Love: a temporary insanity, curable by marriage.

Erma Bombeck

Marriage has no guarantees. If that's what you're looking for, go live with a car battery.

Anonymous

Marriage is when a man and woman become as one; the trouble starts when they try to decide which one.

Anonymous

Adam and Eve had an ideal marriage. He didn't have to hear about all the men she could have married... and she didn't have to hear about how well his Mother cooked.

Jule Renard

Love is like an hourglass, with the heart filling up as the brain empties.

Nick Faldo

We were happily married for eight months. Unfortunately, we were married for four and a half years.

Zsa Zsa Gabor

A man in love is incomplete until he is married. Then he's finished.

Joey Adams

A psychiatrist asks a lot of expensive questions... your wife asks for nothing.

Few One-Liners

It's not true that married men live longer than single men. It only seems longer.

A happy marriage is a matter of give and take; the husband gives and the wife takes.

I haven't spoken to my wife for 18 months--I don't like to interrupt her.

If a man speaks in the forest and there is no woman around to hear him, is he still wrong?

If it weren't for marriage, men would spend their lives thinking they had no faults at all.

I told my wife that a husband is like a fine wine; he gets better with age. The next day, she locked me in the cellar.

Marital Freedom: The liberty that allows a husband to do exactly that which his wife pleases.

Marriage is a romance in which the hero dies in the first chapter.

Compromise: An amiable arrangement between husband and wife whereby they agree to let her have her own way.

Every mother generally hopes that her daughter will snag a better husband than she managed to do...but she's certain that her boy will never get as great a wife as his father did.

No man should have a secret from his wife. She invariably finds it out

Woman like silent men, they think they are listening

Wedding Toasts

Most of us find the task of writing a wedding toast extremely challenging and demanding. To make your speech interesting and memorable you need to add in a punch to it.

These relevant toasts and quotes will make all the difference to your speech.

From the Bride and Groom

May our children be blessed with rich parents!

From the Bride to the Groom or From Groom to Bride

I have known many, Liked not a few, Loved only one. I toast to you.

From the Bride's Mother to the Groom

To the man who has conquered the bride's heart, and her mother's.

To the Bridesmaids

I have a dozen healths to drink to these fair ladies.

From the Bride to the Groom or From the Groom to the Bride

Here's to the prettiest, here's to the wittiest, Here's to the truest of all who are true, Here's to the nearest one,

here's to the sweetest one, Here's to them, all in one -
here's to you.

From the Bride to the Groom

Thank you for all the love you have shown
Thank you for all those good wishes
I'll remember this day when the time it comes
When my husband's at home doing the dishes.
May my groom always walk beside me
May he love me as much as I love him
May our days be spent in sweet contentment
Our loving cup be filled to the brim.

To the Groom

Here's to the groom, a man who keeps his head though
he loses his heart.

To the Bride

May she share everything with her husband, including
the housework.

From the Parents of the Bride and Groom

It is written: when children find true love, parents find
true joy. Here's to your joy and ours, from this day
forward.

To the Gathering

Let us toast the health of the bride; Let us toast the health of the groom, Let us toast the person that tied; Let us toast every guest in the room.

To the Bridesmaids

- A thing of beauty is a joy forever. Here's to these beautiful bridesmaids.

- We admire them for their beauty, respect them for their intelligence, adore them for their virtues, and love them because we can't help it.

From the Groom to the Bride

- She knows all about me and loves me just the same.

- Here's to my beautiful, wonderful bride

- To my folks and her parents too

- Who've made this a day to remember

- Here's to our guests, here's to you!

- May my wife always love me as I love her

- May I love her as much as she loves me

- May we trust and cherish each other

- As long as apples blossom wreathes the tree.

To the Bride and Groom

- Look down you Gods, and on this couple drop a blessed crown.

- Happy marriages begin when we marry the one we love, and they blossom when we love the one we married.

- My greatest wish for the two of you is that through the years your love for each other will so deepen and grow, that years from now you will look back on this day, your wedding day, as the day you loved each other the least.

- It doesn't matter where you get your appetite, as long as you eat at home!

- May the best day of your past be the worst day of your future.

- Marriage: A community consisting of a master, a mistress, and two slaves - making in all, two.

- May the roof above you never fall in and may you both never fall out.

- To the lamp of love - may it burn brightest in the darkest hours and never flicker in the winds of trial.

- May 'for better or worse' be far better than worse.

- The man or woman you really love will never grow old to you. Through the wrinkles of time, through the bowed frame of years, you will always see the dear face and feel the warm heart union of your eternal love.

- May you have many children and may they grow mature in taste and healthy in color and as sought after as the contents of the glass.

- There is nothing nobler or more admirable than when two people who see eye to eye keep house as man and wife, confounding their enemies and delighting their friends.

- Here's to the groom with bride so fair, And here's to the bride with groom so rare!

- Coming together is a beginning; keeping together is progress; working together is success.

- Seek a happy marriage with wholeness of heart, but do not expect to reach the Promised Land without going through some wilderness together.

- Congratulations on the termination of your isolation and may I express an appreciation of your determination to end the desperation and frustration which has caused you so much consternation in giving you the inspiration to make a combination to bring an accumulation to the population.

Here are some Quotes that will enhance the value of your Wedding Toasts

Lord Byron

There is no instinct like that of the heart.

C. S. Lewis

This is one of the miracles of love: It gives... a power of seeing through its own enchantments and yet not being disenchanted.

Mother Teresa

A joyful heart is the inevitable result of a heart burning with love.

Emily Dickinson

That Love is all there is,
Is all we know of Love.

Henry David Thoreau

Love must be as much a light as it is a flame.

Margaret Anderson

In real love you want the other person's good. In romantic love you want the other person.

Robert Heinlein

Love is a condition in which the happiness of another person is essential to your own.

Søren Kierkegaard

Love does not alter the beloved, it alters itself.

Friedrich Nietzsche

When marrying, ask yourself this question: Do you believe that you will be able to converse well with this person into your old age? Everything else in marriage is transitory.

Ice T., The Ice Opinion

Passion makes the world go round. Love just makes it a safer place.

Robert Sternberg

Passion is the quickest to develop, and the quickest to fade. Intimacy develops more slowly, and commitment more gradually still.

Diane Frolov and Andrew Schneider, Northern Exposure, Our Wedding, 1992

Marriage -- It's like a cultural hand-rail. It links folks to the past and guides them to the future.

Friedrich Nietzsche

There is always some madness in love. But there is also always some reason in madness.

Henry David Thoreau

There is no remedy for love but to love more.

Sophocles

One word frees us of all the weight and pain of life: That word is love.

Rainer Maria Rilke

For one human being to love another; that is perhaps the most difficult of all our tasks, the ultimate, the last test and proof, the work for which all other work is but preparation.

Germaine De Stael

Love is the emblem of eternity: it confounds all notion of time: effaces all memory of a beginning, all fear of an end.

Benjamin Disraeli

Romance has been elegantly defined as the offspring of fiction and love.

Jacques Benigne Bossuel

The heart has reasons that reason does not understand.

Barnett Brickner

Success in marriage does not come merely through finding the right mate, but through being the right mate.

Helen Rowland

Falling in love consists merely in uncorking the imagination and bottling the common sense.

J. Krishnamurti

The moment you have in your heart this extraordinary thing called love and feel the depth, the delight, the ecstasy of it, you will discover that for you the world is transformed.

Mother Teresa

It is not how much we do, but how much love we put in the doing. It is not how much we give, but how much love we put in the giving.

Tom Mullen

Marriage -- as its veterans know well -- is the continuous process of getting used to things you hadn't expected.

Andre Maurois

A successful marriage is an edifice that must be rebuilt every day.

Ogden Nash

To keep your marriage brimming, with love in the loving cup, whenever you're wrong, admit it; whenever you're right, shut up.

Victoria Secunda, Women and Their Fathers, 1992

Sons are for fathers the twice-told tale.

Jane Austen

I pay very little regard... to what a young person says on the subject of marriage. If they profess a disinclination for it, I only set it down that they haven't seen the right person yet.

A few more Wedding Toasts to keep up the Wedding Spirits

To the Bride and Groom

May your glasses be ever full.
May the roof over your heads be always strong.
And may you be in heaven half an hour
before the devil knows you're dead.

May your heart be light and happy,
May your smile be big and wide,
And may your pockets always have
a coin or two inside

May your heart be warm and happy
With the lilt of loud laughter
Every day in every way

And forever and ever after.
May your hearts be as warm as your hearthstone.

May your joys be as deep as the Ocean, and your troubles as light as its foam.

May your love be modern enough to survive the times and old-fashioned enough to last forever!

May your refrigerator always be filled with Budweiser, and may all of your ups and down's be under the covers.

May your thoughts be as glad as the shamrocks.
May your hearts be as light as a song.
May each day bring you bright happy hours,
That stay with you all year long.

May your troubles be less and your blessings be more.
And nothing but happiness come through your door.

My wish is that your marriage will be a thing of beauty and a joy forever, always as beautiful as you are today (bride). And may the loveliness of your marriage increase with each year. Here's to the bride and groom.

May we never forget what is worth remembering or remember what is best forgotten.

Remember the love you feel today. Look back on it daily and measure how much it has grown.

May there always be work for your hands to do.
May your purse always hold a coin or two.
May the sun always shine warm on your windowpane.
May a rainbow be certain to follow each rain.
May the hand of a friend always be near you.
And may God fill your heart with gladness to cheer you.

May there be a generation of children
On the children of your children.

May you be friends to each other as only lovers can; and
may you love each other as only best friends can.
May you be poor in misfortune,
Rich in blessings,
Slow to make enemies,
And quick to make friends.

May you both live as long as you want, and never want
as long as you live

May you get all your wishes but one,
So you always have something to strive for.
May you grow old together on one pillow.

May you have all the happiness
and luck that life can hold—
And at the end of all your rainbows
may you find a pot of gold.

May you have food and raiment, A soft pillow for your

head, May you be 100 years in heaven Before the devil
know you're dead

May you have love, health & wealth; but most
importantly, may you have the time to enjoy them all.

May you have warm words on a cold evening,
A full moon on a dark night,
And the road downhill all the way to your door.

May you know nothing but happiness from this day
forward.

May you live each day like your last, and live each night
like your first.

May all your hopes and dreams come true, and may the
memory of this day become dearer with each passing
year.

May all your ups and downs
come only in the bedroom.

May God be with you and bless you.

May the best of your yesterdays be the worst of your
tomorrows
May the blessings of light be upon you,
Light without and light within.
And in all your comings and goings,

May you ever have a kindly greeting
From them you meet along the road.

May the future hold your happiness, May the future
hold your health. May your heart hold your love, and
may your arms hold your babies, yet to come. Here's to
your future happiness together!

May the joys of today
Be those of tomorrow.
The goblets of life
Hold no dregs of sorrow.

May the joys you share today be the beginning of a
lifetime of great happiness and fulfillment

May the light of friendship guide your paths together.
May the laughter of children grace the halls of your
home.
May the joy of living for one another trip a smile from
your lips,
a twinkle from your eye.

May the love you've expressed to each other today
always be the first thoughts during any trying times in
the future.

May the most you wish for
Be the least you get.

May the saddest day of your future be no worse
Than the happiest day of your past.

May you have a family to love you
And friends to stand by your side
And may your good fortune be on the ship
That sails on the incoming tide.

May you always be loved as much as you love
May your blessings be as many as the stars above
May those whom you welcome cross your open door
May you have God's blessing in the years in store

Conclusion

Hope you enjoyed what I had to offer.

Hope that the book has helped you to grow personally and will in some way help you to enjoy your daughter's wedding with much more confidence than what you would have done without it.

Hope it has turned your public speaking fears into challenges and hope you will find your daughter's wedding as an opportunity to have lot of fun and cherish the experience forever.

That's what I have aimed to deliver to you through this book.

Remember giving a speech on your daughter's wedding is an honor. Take pride in it. If you remember the simple rules and practice a little, speech giving is certainly not a complicated affair like creating a space shuttle!

Just take it easy. Believe, you will do well. There is no reason that you will not.

Now is the time to make your daughter feel special, now is the time to show her how much you love her, now is the time to welcome your son in law into the family, now is the time to strengthen the bond of family relations, now is the time to leave a long lasting impression on everyone and now is the time to create some wonderful memories!

Just enjoy the day and have confidence. Everything else will surely fall into place.

Goodluck!

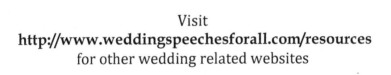

Visit
http://www.weddingspeechesforall.com/resources
for other wedding related websites

CPSIA information can be obtained at www.ICGtesting.com
Printed in the USA
BVOW06s1814140616

452028BV00019B/171/P